SIT DOWN AND DRINK YOUR BEER
Regulating Vancouver's Beer Parlours, 1925–1954

When public drinking returned to much of Canada with the end of prohibition, former hotel saloons were transformed into closely regulated beer parlours, where beer was served in glasses and only to seated patrons. No entertainment was allowed, not even singing, and eventually there were separate entrances and seating for women. The parlours catered to a working-class clientele, and class, gender and sexuality, race, age, and decency were regulated as well as alcohol.

Campbell argues that the regulation of the environment of the classic beer parlour, rather than being an example of social control, is best understood as moral regulation and part of a process of normalization. He focuses on the beer parlours of Vancouver from their beginnings in 1925 to 1954, when liquor laws were liberalized and new venues for the public consumption of alcohol, such as cocktail lounges, were created. Approaching his subject through an examination not only of the state power exercised by the Liquor Control Board, but also of the day-to-day regulation by parlour operators, workers, and patrons, Campbell has written an accessible and original book that will appeal to social historians as well as anyone interested in the history of alcohol and the regulation of leisure.

(Studies in Gender and History)

ROBERT A. CAMPBELL is an instructor in the department of history at Capilano College.

STUDIES IN GENDER AND HISTORY

General editors: Franca Iacovetta and Karen Dubinsky

Sit Down and Drink Your Beer

Regulating Vancouver's Beer
Parlours, 1925–1954

ROBERT A. CAMPBELL

UNIVERSITY OF TORONTO PRESS
Toronto Buffalo London

© University of Toronto Press Incorporated 2001
Toronto Buffalo London

Printed in Canada

ISBN 0-8020-4854-4 (cloth)
ISBN 0-8020-8377-3 (paper)

Printed on acid-free paper

Canadian Cataloguing in Publication Data

Campbell, Robert A., 1952–
    Sit down and drink your beer : regulating Vancouver's beer parlours,
    1925–1954

    (Studies in gender and history)
    Includes bibliographical references and index.
    ISBN 0-8020-4854-4 (bound)   ISBN 0-8020-8377-3 (pbk.)

    1. Drinking of alcoholic beverages – British Columbia – Vancouver –
    History – 20th century.   2. Bars (Drinking establishments) – British
    Columbia – Vancouver – History – 20th century.   3. Drinking customs –
    British Columbia – Vancouver – History – 20th century.   4. Liquor laws –
    British Columbia – Vancouver – History – 20th century.   I. Title.   II. Series.

    HV5310.V35C35 2001   363.4′1′0971133   C00-931971-9

University of Toronto Press acknowledges the financial assistance to
its publishing program of the Canada Council for the Arts and the
Ontario Arts Council.

This book has been published with the help of a grant from the Humanities
and Social Sciences Federation of Canada, using funds provided by the
Social Sciences and Humanities Research Council of Canada.

University of Toronto Press acknowledges the financial support for its
publishing activities of the Government of Canada through the Book
Publishing Industry Development Program (BPIDP).

To Janet

Contents

Acknowledgments

Writing a book is a solitary project, but it is also a collective endeavour that, in my case, includes the assistance of a diverse group of people. I owe much to the staff at the City of Vancouver Archives, the British Columbia Archives, and the University of British Columbia (UBC) Library's Special Collections and University Archives Division. I especially want to thank George Brandak, manuscripts curator at UBC Special Collections. He was both welcoming and helpful during the many weeks that I sat there going through box after box of documents. Versions of some of the material in this book have appeared in *BC Studies* and *Labour/Le Travail*, and I am grateful to the editors of these journals for permission to reprint the material.

This book began as a dissertation at Simon Fraser University, and while I was there I learned a great deal, about history and myself. I particularly want to thank Ian Dyck, Mark Leier, Joy Parr, and Allen Seager. I owe a special debt to Tina Loo, who was my senior supervisor and a wonderful critic in the best sense of the word. Carolyn Strange, the external examiner, made many useful suggestions, and her list initially guided me as I changed a thesis into a manuscript.

People from other institutions read portions of the larger project, and here I thank John Belshaw, Catherine Gilbert Murdock, and Marlene Le Gates. They all helped me to sort out my fuzzy thinking.

Marlene is also a close colleague of mine at Capilano College.

With both paid and unpaid leaves the college encouraged me to complete my studies. While gone, I relied a great deal on Towser Jones to keep me informed. She also encouraged me, especially to finish and to get back to work.

It has been a real pleasure to work with the people at the University of Toronto Press. Their friendly efficiency has continued to impress me throughout this project. I want to give a special nod to Gerry Hallowell. I waited a decade to work with him, and I made it just under the wire before he retired. He had given me sound advice on my first book, even though it was published by another press. I never forgot Gerry's kindness and generosity, and I am sure many authors will miss his him.

Finally, though, it is the personal debts that are the most pleasant to acknowledge. I know my parents, Dorothy and Darrell Campbell, have been puzzled with some of my choices, but they have supported all of them. Quite supportive also have been my in-laws, Jack and Betty Souther. Fortunately I write better than I ski. I owe the most, however, to their daughter, Janet Souther, my wife and partner in many adventures. While I was a student, she paid the bills and held my hand, literally and figuratively. Since then she has endured seemingly endless beer parlour stories, which is more than one should ask of anybody. This book is for her.

Abbreviations

AREC	Alcohol Research Education Council
BCA	British Columbia Archives
BCHA	British Columbia Hotels Association
BCPA	British Columbia Prohibition Association
BCTL	British Columbia Temperance League
BDU	Beverage Dispensers Union
CCL	Canadian Congress of Labour
CVA	City of Vancouver Archives
HRCEBU	Hotel, Restaurant Culinary Employees and Bartenders Union
LCB	Liquor Control Board
RMB-AG	Records Management Branch, Attorney General Files
RSBC	*Revised Statutes of British Columbia*
UBC, SC	University of British Columbia, Special Collections
V&DLC	Vancouver and District Labour Council
VCW	Vancouver Council of Women
VTLC	Vancouver Trades and Labour Council
WCTU	Woman's Christian Temperance Union

SIT DOWN AND DRINK YOUR BEER
Regulating Vancouver's Beer Parlours, 1925–1954

Regulating Public Drinking

For the few Canadian historians involved in alcohol history, temperance and related issues remain the alluring themes. Little historical work has been done in Canada on public drinking in general and public drinking after prohibition ended in particular.[1] This neglect is a real oversight in British Columbia because hotels transformed their saloons into beer parlours after the end of prohibition. The parlour (1925–54) was a reaction to both prohibition (1917–21) and the earlier saloon and as such bears investigation for what it suggests about responses to pro- and anti-drinking sentiments.[2]

At ten cents a glass from 1925 to the late 1950s, the beer in a Vancouver parlour was reasonably priced. A variety of regulations, however, shaped the behaviour and attitudes of those who sat and drank. Parlours regulated their clients' class, gender and sexuality, race and ethnicity, age, and even citizenship. Predictably, and with mixed success, patrons attempted to avoid or alter the regulations. Yet the power of regulation went beyond rules and resistance, for its web enmeshed not only the regulated but also the regulators, a group that included more than state officials. Much of the daily burden of regulation actually fell on the shoulders of parlour operators and workers, who had their own priorities. That regulated drinking environment tells us much about public drinking but also about the society in which the parlours existed.

According to Jack Blocker, 'the task of the historian of alcohol, most generally stated, is to describe and to explain historical patterns of beverage alcohol use and the social response to drinking.' He adds that drinking provides a window on other aspects of society: economic patterns, gender roles, and cultural values.[3] The obvious starting point for assessing alcohol use is drinking itself. Not surprisingly, source material for this often-unremarkable activity is difficult to come by, especially for drinking that occurred beyond the public gaze. In addition, much of the record on drinking has been generated by those who sought to alter, control, or eliminate the drinking patterns of others. We probably know more about working-class drinking habits than about those of elites, in part because of the interests of social historians, but also because working-class drinking tended to be a more public activity and an object of reform.[4] As we see in this chapter, historians have looked at it in terms of class and gender, social control versus culture, and, most recently, moral regulation.

The Poor *Man's* Club?

Since the 1970s the historical literature on public drinking has expanded considerably. Generalizations about such diverse work are problematic, but much of the essence, especially for late-nineteenth-century North America, is captured by the phrase 'the poor man's club.' Most scholars have argued that the pub or saloon was an important part of working-class culture as a centre of male sociability. In addition to good cheer, alcohol, and food, licensed establishments offered entertainment, perhaps accommodation, and such basics as heat and toilets. Depending on time and place, the saloon served as polling place, employment office, and locus of popular politics.[5]

Obviously this characterization of saloon sociability is quite gendered: the poor *man's* club. In her recent study of the American saloon, Madelon Powers emphasizes that saloon culture was 'a masculine domain' where even prostitutes were generally unwelcome. As Thomas Brennan has noted for eighteenth-century Parisian taverns, male sociability meant far more than a desire to associate. Sociability assumed certain values, and 'conviviality imposed certain obligations of consumption and expenditure.' These obligations often brought men into conflict with other societal values, particularly the responsibilities of home and work. Roy Rosenzweig has argued that saloons in Worcester, Massachusetts, were a refuge from both home and work in an era of increasing industrial discipline. The main attraction was not drink but the activities of male companionship: singing, joking, storytelling. At the same time one of the most important bonds of companionship was treating or buying a round of drinks. Powers describes treating as 'an integral part of barroom social interaction.' A treat was not a one-way favour but an expression of honour and mutuality. Even bartenders, who were often forbidden to drink on the job, were obliged to accept a treat or an equivalent, such as a cigar or a snit – a very tiny glass.[6]

In her study of contemporary and Victorian pubs, Valerie Hey argues that pubs reinforced patriarchy through a cult of heterosexual masculinity. Men defined pub space as both public and out of bounds to women. Thus gender dominance was partly expressed by the naming of space. Yet Hey adds that pub culture was based on both males' power and their vulnerability. Their vulnerability was the result of their emotional dependence 'on a desired yet despised gender.' Dominance and desire were closely linked to sexuality. Men attempted to control female sexuality by defining women as deviant if they occupied male space. These comments and the work of other historians of public drinking reinforce the idea of separate spheres, with the public world of drink belonging to men. Female entry was largely restricted to marginalized women.[7]

Many historians have questioned this gender dichotomy. In England, women have had a long history in the drinks trade as brewers, barmaids, and, for widows, licence holders.[8] The practice of granting licences to widows became established in Puritan Massachusetts as a form of poor relief. Yet in nineteenth-century Ontario, women, mainly widows, 'were among the most successful innkeepers,' according to McBurney and Byers. A similar point was made in Edwin Guillet's huge compilation of inns and taverns in pioneer Upper Canada (Ontario): 'Widows – and not always widows of innkeepers – often kept taverns, a fact apparent from the names frequently given to them – "the Widow Brown's Tavern" and "Mother McLean's Inn", among others.'[9] Madelon Powers cites some less forgettable names for places run by female barkeeps, not necessarily widows: 'Peckerhead Kate's,' 'Indian Sadie's,' and 'Big Tit Irene's.'[10]

Perry Duis argues that saloons in Boston and Chicago, rather than being male bastions, were semi-public places that provided some space for women. Boston authorities in particular experimented with various types of gender segregation rather than exclusion.[11] Madelon Powers notes that many American saloons had a separate entrance and area for women, which 'both facilitated and circumscribed women's participation in saloon culture.' Working-class women also 'rushed the growler' – obtained pails of beer from saloons – and drank elsewhere or operated kitchen barrooms.[12] Judith Fingard has shown that in Victorian Halifax some working-class women did drink in saloons and some were proprietors, either of licensed facilities or of illegal home-based operations.[13] Both Kathy Peiss and Roy Rosenzweig have stressed that American saloons, faced with the prohibition movement and commercialized leisure alternatives, tried to become more respectable in the early twentieth century. Peiss concludes, 'Women increasingly frequented saloons.' For England, David Gutzke goes further and claims that the First World War represented the first major shift in popular drinking habits in more than a century. Upper-working-class and middle-class women began patronizing pubs, and a wartime trend became a post-war tradition.[14]

Still, we should not push this argument too far. None of the authors cited fundamentally questions the idea that the world of public drinking was predominantly masculine. Even David Gutzke admits that hostile magistrates, unregenerate regional pub cultures, and unsympathetic maternal feminists prevented gender equality in pubs. As Peiss cautions, women 'penetrated the male sphere of the saloon in ways that were carefully delineated.' For example, they did not stand at the bar, and their presence, particularly as customers, remained controversial. With a slightly different twist, Mary Murphy argues that the public drinking world in Butte, Montana, was thoroughly masculine until prohibition, which 'rattled these patterns' and created public drinking space for women.[15]

Public drinking clearly does not fit a model of simple, separate spheres. While mainly a centre of heterosexual masculinity, it was the site of gender dynamism and even contention. Moreover, a variety of influences may have increased opportunities for public drinking for women in the early twentieth century: 'respectable' saloons, more commercialized and heterosocial leisure, and the destabilizing effects of war and even of prohibition. At the same time, however, we should be cautious about applying these changes to Canada in general and to British Columbia in particular. As Cheryl Krasnick Warsh has commented, by the 1880s public drinking had become unacceptable for respectable women in Canada, and by the turn of the century it 'had vanished as a norm for women.' In British Columbia, by 1910 women were legally banned from saloons. In the analysis of public drinking, specific context is important, and generalizations can take us only so far.[16]

Social Control and Culture

Jack Blocker also has noted that historians of alcohol have adopted two broad interpretations of drinking. The first focuses on social control, in which the state and allied elites 'define the conditions under which ordinary drinking takes place.' The second is a 'cultural model' that 'emphasizes the power of group norms in determining individual drinking behaviour, whether the group is defined by gender, nationality, social class, ethnicity or race.' Blocker argues that historians must use both models to understand drinking and its regulation. Without a doubt, however, social control has been the dominant perspective.[17]

For years now the model of social control has been under attack by some historians. The critique has questioned 'class' as the master category of analysis. Critics have argued that the emphasis on class within the context of social control has pro-

duced narrow, static, and simplistic history. In the words of a
group of feminist Canadian scholars: 'The historical past is far
too complex, and people's lives shot through with too many
contradictions and ambiguities, to be easily captured by this
tired dichotomy of top–down domination versus bottom–up
resistance.'[18]

Scholars influenced by a welter of theories sometimes grouped
as poststructuralist have pushed the debate much further. They
reject the idea of master categories of analysis (such as class,
gender, and race) and the possibility of recreating historical experience. Instead, they focus on the simultaneity and multiplicity of
identities. From this vantage point, social positions are not fixed
or universal. One is at once, for example, a worker, a mother, and
Chinese. The content of these categories varies in relation to
other categories, time, circumstances, and the perceptions of the
observed and the observer. From this perspective it is virtually
impossible to reconstruct the experiences of those who lived in
the past. Instead historical understanding emerges in partial,
fragmented ways through interrogation of categories – the essence of deconstruction. Thus, poststructuralism examines the
power of language, conceived broadly as systems of signification. 'Discourse,' as Tina Loo points out, refers to the 'constitu-
tive and performative role of language; that is, when we talk
about what we actually *do* with language.'[19]

Poststructural critiques have provoked intense debate among
social historians, partly because they challenge the 'primacy of
material conditions in driving or shaping historical subjects and
historical processes.' While the battles continue, other historians
have attempted to bridge the gap between material and discursive orientations by arguing that their opposition is a false dichotomy – the approaches can complement one another. As Laura
Frader has emphasized, discourses contribute to the constitution
of class, gender, and race, but they 'exist in, and in relation with,
the social world and are produced by conscious, acting subjects.'
In a similar manner, Kathleen Canning has argued that the link
between discourse and experience is human agency: 'A notion of
agency as a site of mediation between discourse and experiences

serves not only to dislodge the deterministic view in which discourse always seems to construct experience, but also to dispel the notion that discourses are, to paraphrase anthropologist Sherry Ortner, shaped by everything but the experiences of "the people the text claims to represent."'[20] In short, people and the lives they lived are still worthy of historical investigation.

Moral Regulation

Social historians seeking some more flexible analytical tools have delved into the literature on moral regulation. Much, but not all, of this work is grounded in Foucault's idea of 'governmentality' – 'the contact between the technologies of domination of others and those of the self.' Joan Sangster has described moral regulation as 'the process whereby some behaviors, ideals, and values were marginalized and proscribed while others were legitimized and naturalized.' Moral regulation refers to a process of normalization, the attempt to render natural and obvious what is actually constructed and contested. Ultimately, as Mary Louise Adams has noted, 'Moral regulation limits the forms of expression available to us by masking difference with an illusion of social unity. What are taken for "normal" are, for the most part, representations of dominant interests.'[21] .

Moral regulation is informed by and reinforces knowledge and power. 'Knowledge' here means more than given information that is true or absolute. It is also a process of ordering reality, and its truth is made, not discovered. Moreover, by linking power to knowledge, Foucault broadened conceptions of power to include much more than coercion. 'Power' also refers to the contingent process of creating understandings, of naming. Foucault shifted his gaze away from state coercion and examined power and its effects in the 'capillaries' of society. From this perspective, regulation is a process that involves many actors, including those being regulated. The state is not necessarily the only regulator and is not, some would argue, even the most important one. As well, the state does not act consistently, and the results of state regulation are not always those desired or expected.[22]

Moral regulation is a useful analytical perspective because it blends cultural and control approaches to the analysis of drinking. For example, state officials *did* attempt to impose what I call the 'discourse of decency' on drinkers. Patrons were expected to drink moderately and maintain appropriate comportment. Yet the complexity of class relations inside the parlours challenges simple notions of state-directed control. Parlour workers and operators were charged with much of regulatory enforcement. Sometimes their interests dovetailed with those of the state; often they diverged. Patrons, too, had diverse ideas of what constituted decent behaviour. From the state's point of view, the results of regulation were mixed, uneven, and even contradictory.

Moreover, if we look closely at parlour regulation, much more than class and beer were at work. The 'decent' parlour was also one in which patrons adhered to other dominant norms, especially in regard to gender and heterosexuality. Parlour decency both was informed by these norms and attempted to 're-inscribe' them. Yet decency and deviance were as much a matter of contest and definition as they were fixed categories of behaviour.

Finally, one must conclude that moral regulation and state power are not necessarily in conflict. Parlour regulation certainly went beyond simple patterns of coercion and resistance. It was both informed by and produced particular kinds of knowledge about public drinking. The state remained a powerful regulator, in part because it wove knowledge with coercion.

Outline

These themes are fleshed out in the following chapters, both chronological (chapters 1 and 5) and thematic (2–4). Chapter 1 sets the scene by explaining the origins of the beer parlour. While prohibition was short-lived in British Columbia (1917–21), little support existed for the return of the working-class saloon. Moreover, in the early years after prohibition at least, the issue of public drinking was quite contentious. The beer parlour, introduced in 1925, was designed as a compromise. Those who wanted it could have their glass of beer, but only in a tightly regulated environment devoid of saloon trappings.

In beer parlours the provincial state and its allies tried to engineer public drinking by promoting decency and reducing opportunities for what they considered deviance. Their efforts were conceived in class-specific ways, and chapter 2 emphasizes how concepts of class permeated regulation. While the newspapers often referred to parlours as 'workingmen's clubs,' they were not social centres for the working class in the way in which saloons had been. The official assumption was that working-class comportment needed to be regulated closely.

State resources devoted to regulation, however, were minimal, and parlour operators and workers bore much of the responsibility for enforcement. Their priorities did not necessarily reinforce state priorities, which themselves were not always consistent. Paying close attention to operators and workers allows us to see some of the ways in which class and regulation interacted. Class relations divided operators and workers. Yet both groups were tied, to each other and to the state, in a complex regulatory world that undercut simple ideas of 'them' and 'us.'

Beer parlours also provide a good site to analyse gender relations and sexuality, which is the emphasis of chapter 3. Here, however, I give priority to the patrons, or customers. They had diverse ideas about appropriate comportment and acted accordingly, often despite the efforts of authorities, operators, and parlour workers. Patrons had a real impact on regulation, perhaps best represented by the partitions that operators erected in an only partially successful attempt to isolate unattached men from unattached women.

Most people envisioned the parlour as masculine domain, since public drinking in British Columbia had been primarily a male preserve. Certainly some parlour rituals, especially drinking patterns and treating, contributed to the public markers of heterosexual masculinity. Yet, more important, parlours became a site of gender contention, because, as soon as they opened, some women walked through their doors. Unattached women who entered them were often treated as prostitutes – a label rejected by those women who sought to expand the boundaries of leisure. While women could be condemned for illicit sexuality, men were only chided, provided that actions remained heterosexual.

While official decency embraced heterosexuality, some parlours were gathering places for gay men, lesbians, and transgendered people. Liquor officials did not appear actively to discourage homosexual sociability, as long as it remained confined to certain parlours. Officials, however, did attempt to draw the line when sociability developed into sex in beer parlour toilets.

Not everyone was welcome in beer parlours, and chapter 4 discusses some of the unwanted, especially and mixed-race couples, Asians, minors, and status Indians. Both the definition and the regulation of the unwanted was closely tied to appearance and performance. For example, until 1951 federal and provincial law barred Aboriginal people from any access to alcohol. Yet more often than not waiters and parlour operators determined Aboriginal status by appearance and behaviour rather than by documentation. An Indian was someone who looked or acted 'like an Indian' in the eyes of white men. Those who did not could pass as whites, and in some circumstances Indians were accepted as white. Aboriginal people had much in common with minors, who also were specifically banned from beer parlours. Like Native people, some minors passed through the door. Moreover, as with 'Indian,' 'minor' was a flexible category of regulation, influenced by behaviour and appearance.

No statute prevented Asians or blacks from entering the parlours. Yet de jure and de facto racism was not far below the surface, and racial definition and regulation were not fixed. From the beginning, beer parlour regulations required that licence holders and employees who handled beer be Canadian citizens – that is, eligible to vote. Until after the Second World War that restriction eliminated Asians from either owning a licence or working in a parlour. The restriction was motivated in part by concern that alleged Asian links to vice would compromise the decency of beer parlours. Yet some Chinese were hired in a menial capacity, such as janitor, while others leased hotel rooms, which could be operated separately from parlours.

A few parlours were known for their black patrons, and the authorities particularly watched those establishments. The Liquor Control Board (LCB) also encouraged unwritten house rules that forbade service to mixed-race couples. A man of colour racialized himself – that is, engaged in indecent behaviour – by being in the company of a white woman. The woman, too, sullied 'whiteness' by associating with a man of colour. In terms of regulation, a mixed-race couple was defined as a man of colour with a white woman. A white man and a woman of colour did not constitute a mixed-race couple.

Chapter 5 diverges from the previous three chapters in being more traditionally chronological than thematic. The thematic approach is a useful way to discuss the complexities and multi-level dynamics of regulation, but it can de-emphasize time, especially change over time, which is important to historians, including this one.

The chapter explains the significant post–Second World War changes that culminated in additional licensed facilities by the mid-1950s. We can best understand those changes within the politics of regulation. Yet we must analyse politics in more than one way. It is a state-centred process of balancing interest groups' demands, and in this realm, supporters of cocktail lounges appeared to win. Politics, however, also involves contests that go beyond the state over knowledge about public drinking. After 1945 the discourse of decency shifted, and there emerged what we might call 'a new knowledge' of public drinking. Promoted especially by the press, restaurants, and cabarets, this knowledge emphasized the respectability of cocktail lounges and condemned parlours as indecent, corrupt, working-class centres of excess. Parlours survived, but as even more morally marginalized facilities.

Finally, as we see in the conclusion, parlour regulation says much about the power of the state in civil society. Despite the complexity of regulation and the multitude of regulators, we must not let the state's influence be minimized to a point that obscures the significance of both acquiescence and coercion. Even if one agrees that the authority of the state is fragmented, and power is not just in the hands of the powerful, regulation is not an interactive process among equals. Compliance upheld the values of state regulation and reinforced the knowledge that the state produced. As well, turning a blind eye does not make coercion disappear. The state often could compel people to act in ways that they might not have chosen on their own, even in the apparent chaos of a Vancouver beer parlour.

Chapter One

The Genesis of the Beer Parlour

I first encountered what people then still called a 'beer parlour' in late 1975. I lived in California, but while I was on holiday in Victoria, my cousin, a former railway worker, took me to a local hotel parlour that he occasionally visited. We sat at a round table whose top was wrapped in a terry-cloth cover soaked in beer. Wine was available, but no one seemed to be drinking it. For every round, the waitress always brought us four glasses of beer, each filled to a white line. My cousin referred to the four glasses as railway drinking, which in practice seemed to mean 'Drink a lot quickly.' The beer was cheap – about a quarter per glass – and snack food could not absorb it fast enough. I cannot remember if there was a stripper, but that did not matter because, after much beer, we focused our gaze, as best we could, on a nearby table, where two young women were singing along to the taped music. Glasses in hand, we walked over to them, but they showed no interest in us. So we soon left, and the next morning I felt ill. My grandmother chided me, but I certainly did not regret my adventure.

What I have since learned, however, is that the beer parlour that we visited was different from the ones that I later researched in more traditional ways. The parlours in this book allowed no entertainment, and singing was particularly frowned on. Patrons had to sit in order to be served – by men, as women in general could not be employed. Standing while drinking was forbidden, and a patron could not take a glass to another table. No food of any kind was available, and the only beverage sold was beer. Parlours also physically separated single women from single men. Victoria never had any of these classic establishments because the first beer parlours in the capital city opened only after the rules began slowly to change in 1954.

Saloons

In order to understand the origins and regulation of BC beer parlours, introduced in 1925, one has to know a little about saloons, which dominated public drinking until prohibition during the First World War. Lady Aberdeen, wife of the governor general, recalled her night in a hotel room above a saloon in New Westminster in October 1895:

> At 1:15 H.E. [His Excellency] rang to ask the night porter when the hotel was shut up. 'Not at all,' was the answer. 'When does the bar close?' 'Not at all, Sir.' However it was further explained that this was only the case at the time of the Fair, when there were absolutely no beds available and when therefore the visiting young men were allowed the use of the bar room for the night. They certainly did use it, but happily the singing and shouting were so continuous that I was finally sung to sleep and woke only to hear the carousal being closed by God Save the Queen shortly after 8 a.m.[1]

The experience of Lord and Lady Aberdeen was not as unusual as their night porter tried to make it out to be. In 1880 New Westminster had a licensed bar for every thirteen people. Until 1900 BC saloons were open twenty-four hours a day, seven days a week, and sold all types of liquor. The city of Vancouver was born around a saloon. In 1867 the talkative 'Gassy' Jack Deighton opened the Globe saloon, which was frequented by the sailors and mill workers around Burrard Inlet. The surrounding area, known popularly as Gastown, evolved into the town of Granville. In 1875 four of its ten buildings were 'devoted to selling liquor.' After the new city of Vancouver burned to the ground on 13 June

1886, Tremont House, a popular hotel saloon on Carrall Street, was back in business the next day. By 1888 over 45 saloons existed in the waterfront area.[2]

For those opposed to liquor, saloons were the main target. Prohibitionists rejected the idea of saloons' being working-class centres of good cheer. To the 'drys' they were festering social sores that begat, among other evils, drunkenness, prostitution, and improvidence. Moreover, too much drinking by the lower orders in saloons offered a simple, if simplistic, explanation for the social problems of a rapidly changing society.[3]

Before the First World War, however, the BC drys had only limited success. Their first major campaign was for local option, which would have given individual communities the right to outlaw the retail sale of liquor. Yet because of an unsympathetic Conservative provincial government and a dubious plebiscite in 1909, British Columbia remained the only province without a local-option law. While the plebiscite itself registered a majority in favour of the law, it failed on a technicality – not obtaining the required majority of all those who had voted in the 1909 provincial election. The results give at least some indication of the all-male voters' uneasiness with widespread public drinking. In response, the provincial government in 1911 gave saloons three years to transform their premises into hotels. High capital costs would thus limit their numbers.

War and Prohibition

For the drys the First World War was a turning point. They were able to link their cause with the war effort. Prohibitionists successfully wrapped themselves around the resulting emphasis on efficiency, self-sacrifice, duty, and moral regeneration. In 1915 a small group of Vancouver businessmen organized the People's Prohibition Association. Their goal was to persuade the provincial government to pass a prohibition law and submit it to the voters as a referendum whose results would be binding. By then the winds had shifted in favour of the drys, and in 1916 the government passed a bill that outlawed the sale of liquor except for medicinal, industrial, and sacramental purposes. In September the voters endorsed prohibition and chose a new Liberal government openly sympathetic to prohibition. The British Columbia Prohibition Act went into effect the following October.

Prohibition, however, did not eliminate saloons. On the first day of prohibition, sixty of Vancouver's sixty-nine saloons were open for business. Legally they survived by selling non-alcoholic 'near-beer.' They also sold whatever else they could hide from the inspectors. As the war wound down, support for the dry cause waned, and enforcement became ever more difficult. On a daily basis the most notorious violation was the abuse of medicinal prescriptions for liquor. With a note from the doctor, one could buy liquor from the local druggist, and one doctor wrote some four thousand prescriptions in one month. In 1918 the province created the office of Prohibition Commissioner to improve the increasingly lapsed enforcement. Unfortunately its first occupant succumbed to the temptation of illegally selling liquor, or bootlegging, and he spent two years in jail. By the end of the war many British Columbians had become disillusioned with prohibition.

In 1919 a group of business leaders, some of whom had supported prohibition, organized the anti-dry Moderation League. Rather than favouring a return to private retail sale, the group advocated government control of sealed bottles of liquor and the sale of beer and wine with meals in restaurants. The league did not seek the return of legal public drinking in saloons. Even anti-prohibitionists had to acknowledge the continued success of the drys in undermining support for saloons. Yet the league was confident that the voters would accept their vision of a moderate alternative to prohibition.

The End of Prohibition

Provincial authorities were not so sure. Because of the political volatility of the issue, it did not offer the restaurant option to the voters but simply asked them to endorse either continued prohibition or government control. The drys fought hard to keep prohibition and even brought in prairie firebrand Nellie McClung, who claimed that 'government control would be practically as bad as the days of the open bar.' In October 1920, however, the electorate, which now included women for the first time, overwhelmingly abandoned prohibition in favour of liquor sales in government stores. The first stores opened in 1921, operated by an appointed Liquor Control Board (LCB), which reported to the attorney general.

In order to assuage or deflect criticism from the drys, the strict regulatory tone of government control was set from the start. In order to purchase liquor in a government store a customer needed to obtain a permit, and an annual permit cost nearly a day's wages for the average worker in the early 1920s. Retail prices were high, and the stores themselves were forbidding places, which discouraged lingering or even patronage for that matter. On the outside only a small sign identified the store's purpose, and curtains blocked any view of the interior. Inside, both counters and clerks prevented customers from handling the product until they had filled out written orders and paid in advance. Store vendors also had the authority to limit how much any person could buy.[4]

As for public drinking, the Government Liquor Act of 1921 declared unlicensed public drinking illegal. In order to curb the hotels further, the act also banned the private sale of near-beer. In a legal sense hotel saloons had now been eliminated, but they did not really disappear. In response to the new legislation many Vancouver hotels opened private 'clubs' in their former saloons. Some had membership fees as low as ten cents. Hotel operators claimed that these clubs were perfectly legal, since they were ostensibly closed to the general public and members consumed their own liquor, which they brought with them. The city of Vancouver gave these so-called clubs nominal legitimacy by issuing them business licences. The club veneer did not fool one inspector who claimed in 1922 that the Castle Hotel on Granville Street was 'brazenly selling beer' for twenty to twenty-five cents per bottle.

Veterans' clubs, which wielded much clout after the war, were even more defiant and battled the provincial government in court. Early court decisions favoured the clubs, and in 1923 the government acknowledged the legal setbacks by creating the club licence. What the government could not eliminate it could regulate. The new licence allowed members to store and consume personal liquor on club premises, which were defined as private, not public space. The vast majority of club licences went to genuine veterans' clubs, not the makeshift clubs in hotels.

The club battle showed that the debate over public drinking had not disappeared with the demise of prohibition and the implementation of government control. The debate, both within and outside the legislature, became, if anything, more contentious. New Independent Labour MLA Tom Uphill damned government control as 'class legislation of the worst kind.' The worker's five-cent glass of beer had been replaced by the $3.50 case of beer at the liquor store. Even though both Liberal Premier John Oliver and Attorney General Alex Manson opposed public drinking, they realized that the issue had to be resolved. Their tepid solution was another plebiscite, on beer by the glass.

Led by the renamed British Columbia Prohibition Association, the drys argued that beer by the glass would eventually mean the return of the saloon. The government acknowledged that criticism in the wording of the plebiscite: 'Do you approve of the sale of beer by the glass in licensed premises without a bar under Government control and regulation?' 'Without a bar' was meant to convey the message that a saloon-type environment would not be tolerated. On the wet side the Moderation League was joined by veterans' groups, some labour unions, and the British Columbia Hotels Association (BCHA) – initially a group of Vancouver hotels that had organized to win the right to sell beer by the glass. The wets stressed that beer was a popular drink of moderation that would be sold only under strict regulation. Beer proponents were confident that their views would prevail.

The results on 20 June 1924 surprised many people. Overall in the province dry views carried the day; 73,853 opposed beer, while 72,214 supported it. Fear of saloons, especially in the cities, had not disappeared. Victoria voted against beer, and even Vancouver only barely approved it. Support for beer was strongest in the non-urban areas of the province. While the majority opposed beer, twenty-three of forty electoral districts supported it. Faced with these mixed results, the government, through the LCB, began to license hotel beer parlours in those districts that had supported beer. The first parlours opened in Vancouver in March 1925.

Beer Parlours in Vancouver: Origins and Character

Vancouver's parlours deserve particular attention because that city, as the province's largest, drove liquor policy. It had more parlours than any other city. Liquor authorities hoped that strict supervision of the hotel facilities would reduce criticism of the parlours by dry supporters, who remained politically influential for years. Opponents also targeted parlours in the city. They believed, probably correctly, that if they killed the facilities in Vancouver, they would be victorious across the province.

Nothing in the act or regulations confined beer parlours to hotels, but the BCHA lobbied hard to have 'licences granted to standard hotels only.' In return, hoteliers claimed that they would 'welcome the most stringent regulations.' Hotels had both the facilities and the experience with licensed public drinking. Thus emerged an unwritten partnership between state and industry that lasted for decades. Hotels would have a monopoly over public drinking, but they would accept, in theory at least, a highly regulated drinking environment.[5]

Officially, however, the LCB granted licences to individuals, partnerships, or corporations, not specifically to hotels. In fact, parlour operators rarely owned the hotels in which the parlours were located and in many cases did not even manage the hotel rooms. Hotel owners who received sufficient rent from parlour operators often showed little interest in the room rentals. As a consequence, some 'hotels' were that in name only, despite the unwritten regulation that parlours be part of hotels. Only in 1947 did the LCB receive statutory authority to force parlour opera-tors to gain control over general hotel operations in order to raise standards. At the time nineteen Vancouver hotels had their rooms leased to people not connected with the parlours. Seven years later, when a new liquor act came into effect, the rooms of thirteen hotels were still not under the control of parlour operators.[6]

Vancouver's beer parlours opened in 1925 in former hotel saloons in the downtown core, bounded by Burrard Inlet on the north, False Creek on the south, Burrard Street on the west, and a more elastic boundary at Main Street on the east, with a working-class neighbourhood east of Main being home to a few parlours. The bulk of the parlours' male patrons came from the city's casual labourers, dock, mill, and railway workers, and itinerant loggers. They often stayed in the hotels attached to parlours before they headed back to the woods. A few Vancouver parlours were located in first-class hotels, such as the Devonshire, the Georgia, and the Hotel Vancouver, and they generally attracted little official attention. The LCB framed its expectations and policies in reaction to the lower-end hotels, with their overwhelmingly working-class clientele.

In his semi-autobiographical novel, *Deadman's Ticket*, Peter Trower captured the spirit of the rough environment of Vancouver's beer parlours in the early 1950s: 'The usual crew of tenderloin regulars thronged the sidewalk around me – knots of carousing loggers lurching noisily from bar to bar; shabbily dressed East End housewives looking for bargains at the Army and Navy or the Save-on-Meat store; scrofulous winos with grimy paws cadging dimes in raspy voices; cut-rate hookers wearily heading for toast and black coffee at some greasy spoon cafe; a furtive heroin pusher bound for the Broadway Hotel – Vancouver's notorious "Corner" [Hastings and Main] – to set up shop at a dim beer parlour table.'[7]

Opponents were particularly keen to keep parlours in the downtown area, and during the period under study the LCB accommodated that demand. It allowed no licensed hotels in the more respectable residential areas south of False Creek. Greg Marquis has argued that in Vancouver 'the entire downtown was a segregated district, insulating the more comfortable working- and middle-class residential areas from disreputable behaviour.' His analysis of gambling, prostitution, and illegal liquor concluded that the police and the civic justice establishment were committed merely to managing 'Vancouver Vice,' not to eliminating it. The police knew that the underworld was 'essential to Vancouver's racial and class relations,' as it catered to the desires of the working class and the large Chinese community and provided many jobs as well as civic revenue from fines. Despite what the press and reformers said, Marquis suggests that no consensus existed on vice, so that the police and courts had an ongoing negotiation with it.[8]

While parlours existed in a suspect area, they were also morally suspect places, in part because they were located in hotels. Paul Groth has argued that as early as the 1890s American reformers began to criticize residential hotels as public nuisances. Their main concern was that hotels undermined the family, as they catered primarily to single people. They were especially worried that single working women would be drawn into prostitution, and hotels offered readily available rooms in which they could ply their trade. Reformers censured both rooming-houses, which were home to those who earned a steady but low income, and cheap lodging houses, which sheltered poor transients and day labourers. Many of the hotels in which Vancouver parlours were located were rooming- or lodging houses.[9]

Parlours themselves were also morally suspect. In her study of working-class leisure spaces in Toronto in the 1940s, Mary Louise Adams argued that regulation included the 'discursive constructions of specific types of places as "bad."' Reformers attempted to regulate people by regulating space perceived as immoral. As Adams noted, the reputation of places 'can have a very real, regulating effect on the people who frequent them.' Mariana Valverde has added that the consequence of regulating the drinking environment rather than focusing only on problem drinkers is that indirectly all drinkers are governed. The goal is to 'organize and regulate consumption, producing orderly, disciplined drinking.' One could add that in Vancouver the goal was to produce orderly drinkers as well.[10]

Regulating Beer Parlours

State officials sought to create licensed facilities starkly different from saloons. What constituted the saloon environment, however, was not necessarily clear or fixed. The most potent symbol was the stand-up bar, with its footrail, spittoons, and easy access to the bartender and his liquid wares. Yet, depending on circumstances, the official emphasis could also be on the people, the drinks, the food, or the entertainment. Hence parlours were modelled against what Mariana Valverde has called the 'imaginary saloon,' which allowed officials immense regulatory flexibility and legal elasticity, as they could define almost anything as encouraging a saloon environment.[11]

Parlour regulation took aim at a number of alleged saloon characteristics. The initial one was the name. The Government Liquor Act of 1921 specifically outlawed the public display of the words 'bar,' 'bar-room,' 'saloon,' and 'tavern.' At first the only sign a parlour could display outside was one that read 'open.' In 1933 the government allowed parlours to advertise their presence with the rather vague phrase, 'licensed premises.' The stand-up bar was also a notable proscription. While all parlours had a service bar or counter, no patron could approach it. The liquor act specifically forbade bar service in parlours. In addition the law restricted what could be sold. Until the 1950s beer was the only beverage. Bottled beer was available, but draft beer was the staple trade. In 1926, the first full year of beer service, parlours went through 70,000 barrels of draft beer and the equivalent of 12,000 barrels of bottled beer. Entrenched in statute rather than in the cabinet's more flexible regulations, these restrictions were difficult to alter, as any changes required amending the liquor act.[12] In theory, regulations were more flexible, because changes did not require a vote in the legislature, but in practice such distinctions made little difference. For nearly three decades regulations forbade sale of any food, soft drinks, or even cigarettes in beer parlours. Moreover, the regulations banned all games and entertainment. The unintended irony of these restrictions was that in a beer parlour there was little to do except drink.[13]

Parlour policy was also linked to official conceptions of decency. Everyone, but especially patrons, was expected to behave decently there. No one issued a document that defined it, but in practice 'decency' generally meant moderate consumption, appropriate comportment, and heterosexual propriety. Regulations barred women from working in the parlours, unless they were part of the parlour business. At first, as we see below, many parlours banned women as customers. Soon, however, in concert with the LCB, operators created a separate area for men only and another for women and heterosexual couples. The goal was to separate unattached men from unattached women, which was supposed to enhance decency by discouraging prostitution. These areas became more rigidly separated by partitions erected during the Second World War, and regulators devoted a great deal of attention to preventing unattached men from crossing over to the ladies and escorts' side.[14]

Despite the emphasis on legal regulation, much of official policy on parlours was the product of LCB discretion rather than of statute or regulations. These policies covered a wide range of activities. For example, waiters took beer on trays to small tables, and customers had to remain seated to drink, even though sitting was not a legal requirement. The LCB also discouraged booths and settees, because of the opportunities they provided for more intimate contact. The act and regulations never entrenched gender segregation, which existed as 'instructions from the Board.' When queried by a parlour operator about these unwritten rules in 1949, the chairman responded, perhaps as a veiled threat, that if all the rules were official more licences would be suspended for violations. He added that the 'instructions' dealt with 'minor items' – a somewhat disingenuous claim, considering the priority given to gender segregation.[15]

The human resources devoted to regulation appeared to be minimal. The LCB itself was a small organization based in Victoria, its office a short walk from the Parliament Buildings. From the outset of government control in 1921 the three-member board was plagued by liquor and patronage scandals. They undermined the board's credibility and effectiveness for years, despite new members and a new Conservative government in 1928. Real stability arrived only in 1932, when William F. Kennedy was named the sole member and chairman of the LCB. Kennedy, a former Conservative MLA, had served on the board since 1930. Charges of corruption and patronage continued to haunt the board, but Kennedy loyally served several governments and a variety of attorneys general. Only death removed him in August 1951. His successor, Col. Donald McGugan, had been employed by the board since 1923, for most of the time as deputy chairman. McGugan kept his new post until his retirement in 1969.[16]

On the enforcement side, the chairman worked closely with the board's secretary and the chief inspector, who was responsible for the inspectors. At the end of the 1920s Vancouver had sixty-three beer parlours, but there were only three parlour inspectors for the entire province. By the late 1940s about that many watched only Vancouver, and the number of parlours remained the same. The LCB's enforcement resources also included a few undercover agents, who tried to maintain their anonymity by signing their reports with numbers rather than names.[17]

Parlour regulation resulted in quite a paper trail. One of the richest sources for the parlours is the inspector's reports. As one might expect, the bulk of the material is official LCB documentation, particularly annual inspection reports and related correspondence. Yet the files collectively contain information from a range of sources: reports by undercover investigators and police; correspondence from the Division of Venereal Disease Control, hotel associations, and unions; letters of complaint; fire wardens' summaries; newspaper clippings; comments from temperance groups and from employees; and summaries of phone calls. Some files are quite thin, but others – the ones that dealt with problem parlours – go on for hundreds of pages.[18]

In addition to providing a lot of information, these files show that parlour regulation extended beyond those employed by the LCB. Formally and informally, the police, health officials, and temperance observers assisted the board. The press also played a regulatory role, for the newspapers had quite an appetite for alleged debauchery and corruption in and around parlours. An unfavourable newspaper story about a particular establishment usually resulted in an immediate visit from an inspector. Since parlours were inspected regularly only once each year, on a daily basis much of the regulatory burden fell on operators and workers. Finally, as odd as it sounds, inertia became a form of regulation. Because public drinking remained a contentious issue, any changes would alienate some vocal group. Thus, until the 1950s, the status quo was a regulatory priority.

In a sense, then, as George Chauncey argues, liquor licensing made state regulation both less visible and more pervasive. The threat of suspension or cancellation of licences certainly encouraged parlour operators and employees to act as regulators. Mariana Valverde goes even farther – too far, really – with her claim that the ultimate target of liquor regulation was not the drinker but the licence holder. Government 'subcontracted' regulation of drinkers to the licence holders. Yet, as Valverde admits, regulation was not as simple as subcontracting implies. Operators had an economic interest in promoting drinking as well as one in protecting their licences. Moreover, the state's interest in 'highly moralized techniques' was never far from the forefront of regulation, and these techniques were directed mainly at patrons.[19]

The environment of the beer parlour was closely linked to the saloon and prohibition. In a sense the parlour was a reaction to both. The drys had undermined the view of the saloon as an acceptable social institution, and that legacy remained even after prohibition had succumbed to the demand for the return of legal liquor. The implementation of government control, however, did not offer an obvious solution to the prickly issue of public drinking, and the plebiscite of 1924 showed that people continued to have divergent views on the subject. The beer parlour did not emerge as a completely hatched compromise, although some key elements, such as the absence of a bar, were present from the beginning. Yet it took shape fairly quickly, as the emphasis was on a highly regulated environment. Officials were determined that the parlour would not evolve into a saloon. It would be a different institution, one that would promote decency, not undermine it.

Chapter Two

Operators and Workers: The Ties That Bind

The *Official Handbook* in 1950–1 for Local 676 – the beer parlour workers' union – offered a pointed juxtaposition. In it the local's president did not shy from the language of class struggle. He stated that 'the true goal of Unionism' was 'to put a stop to the exploitation of the workers.' Yet the volume also contained a photograph of the president of the union's local joint executive board making a presentation to the retiring president of the hotels' association. At the initiative of Local 676, the chief executive of the employers' organization received a lifetime membership in the international union.[1]

From the beginning in 1925, state officials, the press, parlour operators and employees, and even patrons conceptualized beer parlours in class terms. Working-class parlours were the successors to working-class saloons, though an intended pale version of them. Class permeated the entire discourse of regulation, from beer as the working man's drink to the behavioural expectations that state regulators had of patrons and workers. Yet because of the priority given to regulation, class operated in complex ways in beer parlours. At one level the relationship between entrepreneurial parlour operators and their unionized workers would seem to fit a two-class model, and to a certain extent it did, but, as the photograph described above shows, life was not entirely that simple. In order to explain some of these complexities, I want to explore in this chapter the working world of operators and workers – their association and their local, respectively; the roles of gender and of class; and the dimensions of regulation, as exemplified in the responses to gambling, violence, and the beer shortage of the Second World War.

Local 676 and the BCHA

On 5 May 1925 the Vancouver Trades and Labour Council (VTLC) received the credentials of the newly named Beverage Dispensers Union (BDU). By the beginning of September Tim Hanafin of the BDU reported that all of Vancouver's parlours had been organized. This achievement was notable for a union that had endured much hardship during prohibition. Union folklore credited Hanafin's efforts in the dry years for keeping the union an affiliate – Local 676 – of the Hotel & Restaurant Employees & Bartenders International Union.[2]

Local 676 had received its charter as a bartenders union in July 1903, and it prospered in the years before prohibition. While most of Vancouver's hotel saloons survived prohibition, they certainly did not thrive during the dry years. From a bartender's point of view one of the many unfortunate consequences of prohibition was the reduction of regulation. For example, since near-beer technically was not liquor, at first anyone could sell it. Numerous non-union 'jitney bars,' named after the private automobiles that competed with taxis, opened on Vancouver streets. The competition hurt. By 1918, Local 676 had changed its name to the Soft Drink Dispensers, and the union discussed amalgamation with the restaurant workers.[3]

For bartenders, the opening of beer parlours meant a return to the preferred environment of regulated public drinking. Union bartenders had much incentive to support the hotel operators in their successful bid to restrict beer sales to hotel parlours and thus unionized workers. Local 676 became one the strongest defenders of the hotel monopoly, and to a large extent workers linked their fortunes with those of their parlour employers. Structural conflict did not disappear, but it was sometimes difficult to see.

Regulation of beer parlours resulted in different work processes from those in saloons. The primary responsibilities of the
man behind the counter were pulling beer, hooking up kegs, and
minding the till. His other duties were oriented to regulating
patrons – for example, preventing unattached men from entering
the area reserved for women and couples. Still, the counter worker
was not a bartender in the style of the old saloon, and the collective agreement acknowledged this difference with the title of
'tapman.'[4]

Moreover, since bar service was prohibited, parlours needed
more waiters. They bridged the distance between customers and
tapmen. Waiters had the initial responsibility of deciding if patrons were at least twenty-one-years old, non-Aboriginal, sober,
and located on the correct side of the parlour. Waiters were
supposed to take orders and place them at the bar. Yet they often
bought a tray of beer from the tapman and sold it on demand,
which the inspectors considered 'pushing' beer. While a waiter
had the most contact with abusive customers, he also had more
opportunity for sociability, even if officially he could not accept
tips. Monitoring tipping was very difficult, but its being banned
from the beginning was a warning to waiters not to encourage
excessive consumption and hence increased income through tips.[5]

Working in a busy parlour was physically demanding, particularly for the waiters. A consultant hired by the hotels in 1957 to
estimate potential profitability calculated that one tapman could
service six waiters. If he worked at his theoretical maximum, he
would pull 1,800 glasses an hour, or one glass every two seconds.
The consultant also concluded that a waiter could oversee nine
tables, and theoretically he could make fifteen rounds per hour
and serve 300 glasses of beer. Until the 1950s the standard full
beer tray held twenty glasses, which, according to the union,
weighed 22½ pounds. In an hour, then, a waiter might carry
nearly 340 pounds of beer in glasses. The consultant admitted
that his calculations might not be 'humanly possible.' Even at a
fraction of these rates, however, a busy waiter would be almost
run off his feet. As a result, many waiters aspired to be tapmen.
The work was less physically challenging, and the pay was better.[6]

Parlour workers operated under a master collective agreement negotiated between Local 676 and the British Columbia Hotels Association (BCHA). For the union the strongest article of the agreement was its closed-shop provision, which offered some workers' control. Technically, parlours could hire only workers dispatched from the union office. The closed shop was not water-tight and was violated by both operators and workers. Yet the union keenly defended it, and, judging from the occasional flare-ups over the issue at union meetings, so did most members. Once a man achieved the status of 'steady' at a hotel, he no longer had to deal with the union dispatcher. Casual men were the ones commonly sent from the union office.[7]

Seeking more control over hiring, the BCHA tried to eliminate the closed-shop provision. In a brief to a conciliation board in 1953, it argued that the closed shop had 'proved very unsatisfactory to the Employer.' The BCHA claimed that the union often sent workers who were ignorant of the regulations and engaged 'in the nefarious trade of taking bets on duty, drinking on duty, smoking on duty, all of which is [sic] contrary to regulations.' Drinking on duty had long been a concern of the BCHA because of pressure from the LCB and complaints from operators. The exasperated manager of the Anchor Hotel in 1951 blamed a spare waiter for his parlour's latest incident of drinking on duty. In a postscript to a formal explanation to the LCB he scribbled: 'We call the Bev. Dispensers Union nearly every day for waiters and have never or hardly ever been sent efficient Help.'[8]

Spare workers were easy and common targets, but the union executive also was concerned about drinking, since it jeopardized the closed shop. After a tapman was caught drinking at the Regent in 1948, the union's business agent discreetly informed the LCB that he had been called to the hotel many times to check on employees' drinking. According to union records, the Regent went through twenty-nine men in less than a month in search of crew that would not drink on the job. He suggested that the government take action and fine the individuals. The board's chief inspector eschewed more use of state authority and told the union that it should regulate its own members by putting offenders 'before a disciplinary Board of the Union and fining them accordingly.'[9]

. The executive began punishing delinquent members, but drinking at the union office, during union meetings, and before or on the job remained vexing problems. In 1958 the local supported a recommendation from the executive to create a trial committee to deal with infractions. Members could be fined, suspended, or both, and a suspended member could not work. The local later prepared a list of rules to guide men sent by the dispatcher. The union could discipline them if they drank on the job or, for that matter, gained employment 'without being dispatched from the Union office.' In 1965 two members of the executive secretly met with Attorney General Robert Bonner. According to him, they said that the collective agreement bound them to dispatch men even if their 'performance, by reason of their taste for liquor, is going to be unsatisfactory.' The attorney general told the LCB's chairman that the union sought LCB assistance 'to police their shop.'[10]

Gender and Class

The working world of operators and workers was predominantly, but certainly not exclusively, masculine. Some women, such as Mrs Rose Low, held beer licences. Low opened the Empire Hotel parlour on East Hastings in 1925 and remained there until 1931. She moved on to the Martinique Hotel and in 1935 served on the executive of the BCHA. By 1938 she was the licensee of the Clarence Hotel. In 1948 Mary Rosen became the sole licence holder of the Stratford parlour after buying out her male partner. As well, in 1948 Mrs N. Fabri and Miss I. Anderlini were the sole directors of the Europe Hotel. These cases were unusual only in that these women were the sole licensees. By the 1940s almost all beer parlours were small, private corporations, and between 1948 and 1954 women served as directors in at least twenty-four Vancouver parlours. Women owned or co-owned a few hotel buildings, and some leased their room operations to women.[11]

While the regulations generally banned female parlour workers, a woman who was part of the business could work on the premises. Yet even where women were the sole licence holders, their names do not appear on the lists of people who regularly handled beer. In a 1961 conciliation brief, Local 676 made reference to 'one case in point where an operator works, and has his wife also take part in the operation, ... thus displacing a bartender and a waiter.' This example, however, was the exception, not the rule. The only women who were regularly employed in Vancouver parlours were janitors, and they generally worked when parlours were closed. Outside Vancouver, women servers were more common, but they tended to be part of family-run operations. As well, hotels in the BC interior did not have the high profile of those in Vancouver, and not all had collective agreements. Depending on how one ordered reality, 'woman server' could mean a threat to unionized male labour, a method of reducing costs, or a symbol of family and community in a small town.[12]

Class divisions obviously separated workers from parlour operators. Operators were entrepreneurs who tried to maximize their profits, while workers were unionized employees who sought to improve their wages and conditions and exert some control over their working lives. Every year or two the conflict was resurrected, at least rhetorically, in the negotiations between the BCHA and Local 676. During the period under study, however, not a single strike or lockout occurred.

While the class divide was real, it was not fixed. Some employees, especially tapmen, served as parlour managers, with the authority to hire and fire. Some employees became operators. A.J. 'Jack' Galloway is a particularly interesting, if unusual, case. From 1937 to 1951 he was manager and tapman at the Belmont, except for his time away on war service. In 1952 he sought to become a director of the Dominion Hotel, and later that year he was elected president of Local 676 – a post that he held a couple of times in the 1950s. In the early 1960s, while still on the executive of Local 676, he started a controversial bar school as a private enterprise that was closely linked with the union.[13]

Some operators, particularly in the smaller hotels, worked in the parlours, usually behind the service counter. Local 676 was constantly trying to restrict the number of operators who could work in the parlour. In 1953 the union's business agent informed the LCB that if an operator was allowed to work in a parlour 'the ultimate result could be an Union employee out of a job.'[14]

Sometimes operators invoked class to explain conditions in their parlours. In 1953 the operator of the New Empire said that his parlour had problems because 'the clientel [*sic*] in our district consists of loggers and miners and at times are hard to handle.' Yet justifications based on class occasionally went in the other direction, too. In a letter supporting the Devonshire Hotel's application for a beer licence, T.E. Chester of the Hotel Vancouver said that patrons of 'first-class hotels' were not 'accustomed' to 'the surroundings provided by the majority of licensed premises.' Hence, upscale hotels such as the Devonshire and the Vancouver needed their own beer licences so that their customers could avoid working-class parlours and patrons.[15]

Liquor inspectors also walked through parlour doors with expectations grounded in class. Only rarely, however, did they express these views in overt political terms. For example, in 1952 an undercover agent in the St Helena Hotel 'noticed three men circulating among patrons a petition sponsored by the Communist Party ... against an increase in bus fares.' He ended his report: 'No other infractions were observed.' Three days later an inspector met with the operator to discuss the petition. His concern was the presence of Communists, not the opposition to the bus fare increase – an issue later taken up by the respectable Vancouver Council of Women.[16]

More commonly, the class concerns of inspectors were linked to behavioural expectations. In most parlours, inspectors were prepared for a rough crowd, and they seemed surprised when they did not find trouble. After touring the Melbourne Hotel in February 1928 an inspector commented that 'considering that this premises caters largely to the Longshoremen trade and Fishermen, the patronage is kept pretty well in hand.' A quarter-century later an inspector's report on his tour of six downtown eastside hotels echoed these sentiments: 'Considering the influx of loggers and construction men ... at this time of year for the Christmas Holidays, conditions were fairly orderly throughout the east end of the city.'[17]

More typical, at least in terms of expectations, was an inspector's description of the New Fountain in 1951: 'I arrived to see a fight started in the Men's section ... [sic] in which one of the participants was being kicked across the floor.' The inspector asked the manager if he intended to stop the fight and recorded the manager's reply as, 'Well! that's nothing, that goes on all the time.' When the inspector pulled out his identity card, the manager 'immediately jumped in to quiet the gang down.'[18]

The inspectors also tried to enforce the ban against games, dancing, and music, including singing, all of which they believed encouraged a saloon-like atmosphere and excessive camaraderie. Singing caused the most problems for the board because patrons' voices were difficult to regulate, and some operators condoned it. A convivial atmosphere, with thirst-inspiring songs, could increase beer sales. Usually parlour operators were just warned about singing. In March 1951 an inspector standing on the sidewalk outside the Dominion Hotel on Abbott Street observed 'mass singing by the patrons in the ladies's section of the licensed premises, the leader apparently being Mr [E.M.], licensee, who had a megaphone and was moving from one table to another. At intervals he handed the megaphone to the patrons, who continued to sing.'[19] According to the chief inspector, the operator claimed that he used the megaphone only for calling customers to the telephone, and 'when questioned in regard to patrons singing through it, he stated, "They took it away from me."' The LCB took his licence away for ten days. The BCHA then posted signs in parlours that warned patrons against singing and playing musical instruments. Yet with ingenuity and defiance customers still sang, sometimes with the assistance of operators.[20]

Regulation

While class relations divided operators and workers, they were part of a regulatory world that entwined workers and operators, their allies in the union and hotel association, and the LCB. In the web of regulation the state did not manipulate all the strands. By examining violence, gambling, and the Second World War beer shortage we can see how regulation operated at different levels simultaneously.

Violence

Violence in beer parlours consisted primarily of fights among patrons, between patrons and workers, and between patrons and operators. Not surprisingly, the board showed the most interest in fights that were captured in the press or attended by police. In June 1952 an inspector was immediately dispatched to the Broadway Hotel after both the Vancouver *Sun* and the *News-Herald* reported on a four-man fight that resulted in two broken chairs, thirty smashed beer glasses, and the arrest of all four men. The police claimed that the fight was a result of 'two rival groups arguing over narcotics.' The inspector noted that the glasses were broken as a result of parlour workers' trying to remove the fighting patrons. Because no one was drunk and the fight began almost spontaneously, the inspector did not blame the parlour. He did suggest, however, that 'when known "hop heads" attempt to enter their premises they should be barred and refused service.'[21]

Encounters between patrons and workers or operators most often were a result of patrons' being ejected. The consequences could be tragic. In 1948 the operator of the New Empire parlour was charged with manslaughter after he struck a patron who had apparently interfered with the ejection of another patron. The struck customer fell to the sidewalk, fractured his skull, and died the next day. The operator was later acquitted. A similar incident occurred in 1953 when a man died after being tossed from the St Regis by a waiter. The waiter was charged, but the charge was dismissed for lack of evidence.[22]

Although the inspectors did not always identify gender, fights most commonly involved men against men. Yet it was not exceptional for women to participate. In one incident an undercover agent used a punctuation mark to express his disdain for a victorious woman: 'one lady ? striking her boyfriend, giving him a bloody nose.' Another example involved an off-duty police officer at the Anchor Hotel in 1953. The inspector reported that 'Mrs. [A] had thrown a beer glass at her husband and had hit a lady, Mrs. [W] who was sitting at an adjoining table on the forehead, which resulted in Mr. [W's] getting up and calling Mrs. [A] a name and giving her a slap.' The police were called but took no action, perhaps because Mr W. was a police officer. When the inspector tried to interview him, he was told that the officer was on vacation and had 'apparently left the city.'[23]

The LCB consistently made it clear that it expected operators and workers to control violence. After a 1952 encounter at the Columbia Hotel in which a man tried to hit his wife and in turn had his jaw broken by another man, the inspector concluded that the parlour needed a floorman 'to keep better supervision as this hotel is situated in a very tough part of town.' After a complex incident at the Stanley Hotel the same year in which a woman pulled the hair of a doorman who was pushing her husband, the operator asked the inspector what he should do. The inspector replied that 'it was strictly a matter between himself and the grieved party.'[24]

We can see tthe LCB's expectations in a bizarre incident at the Lotus Hotel on Abbott Street in April 1953. In response to a newspaper story about a shooting there, an inspector went to the Lotus. He learned that a man had entered the parlour, ordered two beers, and then pulled out a gun and fired a shot into the ceiling. Apparently knowing his duty, a waiter approached the man, who fired another shot into the ceiling and then ran out. The parlour operator then phoned the police, and the man was later arrested elsewhere. The inspector did not comment on the waiter's brave, as well as foolhardy, action; he simply concluded, 'Submitted for information purposes.' His boss also took little notice of the waiter and scribbled 'no further action' on the inspector's report.[25]

Much of the burden of regulating violence fell on waiters because they had the most direct contact with customers and because doormen and floormen came from their ranks. Local 676 told a conciliation board that employees deserved compensation for damaged clothing as a result of 'additional duties,' which included 'stopping fights in licensed premises and ... ejecting drunks and undesirables. Many a time our people wind up get-' ting the worst of it, such as a black eye, or our clothing torn off.' Sometimes they suffered even more. For example, in 1952 two waiters were beaten up after work outside the Princeton Hotel. The parlour manager asked one waiter to lay charges against his assailant, and, when the waiter refused, he fired him.[26]

Regulating violence put high expectations on waiters. The first edition of Local 676's handbook, in 1949, contained a section called 'Judo For Self Defence,' which claimed that 'judo is an ideal sport for waiters.' With judo, a waiter could 'handle any rowdy' without causing pain and with a 'minimum of fuss or disturbance.' The purpose of judo, however, was to 'keep the situation in hand – not drive away business.' Waiters had to know when to act, whom to act against, how much force to use, and when to bring in the authorities. How willingly waiters engaged in regulating violence is an open question, but their union accepted that role for them, and the LCB expected their co-operation.[27]

Gambling

With gambling, the LCB relied less on parlour workers and operators to regulate it because the board suspected that they often participated themselves. The board's main concern was the placing of bets on horse racing, or bookmaking. Betting away from the track was illegal, but it was one of the most common vices in the city. Some bookmakers worked out of beer parlours, while others relied on 'runners' to gather bets in parlours.[28]

After the Second World War the LCB took an even keener interest, when authorities became increasingly concerned that some operators and employees were bookmaking. The LCB worked closely with the police and the BCHA to suppress the activity. In a 1948 letter the chief inspector informed the chief of

police: 'The whole matter of bookmaking has been fully discussed with the hotelmen and the Board, and it is felt that in
many instances it is impossible to stop runners operating in beer
parlours. In many cases, the licensees are unaware that their
staffs are working in collusion with bookmakers or runners.
There are, of course, several instances where this element is more
or less welcomed for the purposes of drumming up trade.'[29]

The chief inspector's concern about 'collusion with bookmakers' was more justified than he realized, and the collusion went
beyond parlour workers and operators. Walter Mulligan, chief of
police from 1947, was removed from office in October 1956, just
before he was to appear before a public inquiry into allegations
that the chief had been accepting bribes from bookmakers for
years.[30]

While complaints about bookmaking involved at least a dozen
hotel parlours, the police and the LCB worried particularly about
a handful. The one that attracted the most attention was the
Lotus Hotel. In 1946 the police informed the LCB that they had
received complaints about bookmaking there. Twice when police
officers entered the parlour 'a waiter has been heard to shout an
alarm or warning,' and 'during the past month a "look-out" man
has been standing in the doorway.' The police claimed that the
majority of customers were reading racing literature and that a
bookmaker was 'working with consent and approval of the management.' In October 1948 John Moffat, who was not an employee, was convicted of bookmaking, and a few days later the
Lotus had its beer licence suspended for ten days.[31]

Moffat was active again at the Lotus in 1950, and reports about
bookmaking flowed in from the LCB's undercover agent. Moffat
recorded bets on the back of a cigarette case, so he could quickly
rub them off if need be. In July 1951 he was again convicted of
bookmaking after he took bets from two police officers in plain
clothes. The chief inspector concluded, 'The bookmaker and his
runner were known not only to the management, but also to the
staff.' A few days later the Lotus again had its licence suspended.[32]

Some operators did cooperate with the LCB, especially once

bookmaking became apparent in their premises. In November 1948 a bookmaker was observed in the Abbotsford Hotel, and he 'recorded bet from waiter each time.' After a warning letter from the chief inspector, the parlour manager barred the bookmaker and fired the waiter. In another example from the Royal Hotel, Mrs I.R. wrote the LCB in September 1950 to complain that she had been refused service because the operator accused her of 'taking bets on the horse races while in there.' She admitted that she had 'placed bets quietly,' but 'never to so to speak make book.' She also enjoyed reading the racing form over a beer in the Royal. According to the inspector, the operator refused to serve her because she was the friend of a barred bookmaker, and he suspected that she 'was taking a few bets.' The inspector concluded that since the parlour had been warned about bookmaking, the operator 'was making every effort to eliminate all possible suspects, refusing service, as in this instance.'[33]

LCB officials probably never expected to eliminate bookmaking from Vancouver parlours, just as they knew that some fighting would occur. Their leaving operators and workers to regulate violence may have reflected their acknowledgment that it was best not to contest what they could not control. As long as violence did not attract too much attention from police or press, its main impact was on those involved. Parlour workers, especially waiters, carried the burden of regulating the fights that occurred largely within the working class.

Bookmaking was different because the LCB believed, and could marshal some evidence to show, that workers and employers together were engaged in it. Perhaps LCB officials were troubled by this cross-class alliance in deviance, but bookmaking had more potential than fighting to undermine official authority. Bookmakers provided a direct link between the parlours and the city's underworld. In parlours all forms of gaming were illegal, even those that did not involve betting. The LCB concentrated not on the patrons who illegally played poker or checkers, but rather on the gambling that moved people in and out of parlours and effectuated the broader connections with the criminal world.[34]

The Wartime Beer Shortage

During the Second World War parlours experienced a shortage of beer because of rationing and a growing population. In response some tapmen poured short glasses of beer, and that action provoked a howl of protest from patrons. Organized labour, the parlours, and the LCB all emphasized the gender and particularly the class dimensions of the shortage. The shortage underscored the limits of state regulation, and in this case operators and workers colluded to undermine that authority.

Especially outside British Columbia, temperance support increased during the war because dry leaders tied their cause to wartime efficiency and productivity. At its annual convention in May 1940 the British Columbia Temperance League (BCTL) urged the provincial government to close 'all beer saloons and places of public liquor treating and drinking during the war.' Linking parlours to 'saloons' and 'treating' summoned images of the pre-prohibition bars during the First World War. In October 1941 the Canadian Temperance Federation lobbied the federal cabinet to invoke the War Measures Act to stop 'the sale of alcoholic beverages in taverns, beer-rooms, wine shops, etc.' As measured by polls, public opinion became more sympathetic to the temperance message, particularly as the war worsened in 1942. That December Ottawa reduced the quantity of beer available for sale and asked provinces to reduce hours of retail sale.[35]

Even before this action, the hotels moved to defend parlours. In a brief to the provincial attorney general, the BCHA described the beer parlour as 'a workmen's club,' similar to a British pub. As a low-alcohol, 'pure and uncontaminated product,' beer caused no harm. In fact, beer drinking could actually help improve wartime efficiency by maintaining workers' morale. The BCHA also warned that, 'particularly among workers,' there was 'irritation with regulations which they do not understand and the necessity for which as a war measure is not apparent.' The Hotel Association of Canada expressed similar sentiments. It claimed that the British government had found, 'by actual tests, that the workman produces more goods when his drinking habits are not interfered with by legislation.'[36]

The province, however, adopted general liquor rationing before the federal government. It was minimally influenced by temperance pressure, but its more immediate concern was dwindling provincial liquor supplies and a population growing rapidly because of the influx of shipyard workers and military personnel. In November 1942 it announced that beer parlours' hours would be reduced from thirteen to eleven each day; the LCB shaved off thirty minutes at the beginning and at the end of the drinking day, and it also imposed a one-hour closing at suppertime. It sought thereby to encourage drinkers to go home and stay there. The LCB's chairman informed the secretary of the BCTL that 'while we cannot be accused of denying the working man his right to beer if he so desires, nevertheless it [supper-hour closing] will be the means of breaking up the period of drinking.' Early in 1943, as a result of the federal limits on supplies, the province restricted parlours to 80 per cent of the quantity of beer that they had sold the previous year. It further reduced parlours' hours to eight: 2 p.m. to 6 p.m. and 7 p.m. to 11 p.m.[37]

Organized labour reacted harshly to restrictions on beer, and unions and trades councils fired off complaining letters to the LCB. In February 1943 the Vancouver and District Labour Council (V&DLC), successor to the VTLC, endorsed a resolution that called beer restrictions 'a clear ruling leading to class distinction. The working man needs and looks forward to his beer and in most cases does not want and cannot afford to buy hard liquor on a worker's pay.' The next month it went further and protested the restrictions 'in a world run amock [*sic*] over who shall own and control the surplus values produced by the working class.' The council stopped short of supporting a 'No Beer No Bonds' proposal, which would have meant that unless more beer became available, workers would not buy war bonds.[38]

The BC beer shortage also became an issue at the Canadian Congress of Labour (CCL) convention in Quebec City in September 1943. Delegates from Vancouver claimed that it was often impossible to get a beer in Vancouver after 'six or seven o'clock in the evening,' as parlours often quickly sold their daily allocation. A resolution passed by the convention noted that if 'essential war workers' had more beer, 'morale and production brought about by these workers would be greatly increased.'[39]

The shortage of beer inspired more specific concerns about the decreasing amount in each glass. Workers complained of 'short glasses' caused by too much head, or foam. Short glasses also reflected operators' desire for profit. Both levels of government increased taxes on beer during the war. While the breweries initially absorbed some of the burden, they passed most on to the beer parlours, but operators were not allowed to raise the retail price. Operators reacted in two ways. First, they reduced the size of the glasses. The LCB did not legally require a specific size, but since the 1930s it and the BCHA generally had agreed to eight ounces. During the war the typical glass shrank to 7.25 ounces, with the board's tacit approval. Second, some operators told their tapmen to pour less beer and more foam, which they could easily do by changing the angle of the glass while pouring.[40]

Short service became an increasingly common complaint. In July 1943 the V&DLC's executive met with the secretary of the BCHA, who told the labour leaders that the hotels considered the problem 'a serious matter.' He later sent the labour council a copy of a special warning to BCHA members about short service. Yet the BCHA's action had little impact on some of its members, as by April 1944 the LCB was flooded with complaints from workers who condemned glasses filled with more head than beer. The board told the BCHA that it simply must stop short service. The BCHA's secretary again informed his members that 'the working man ... is entitled to his full glass of beer, as is everyone of our customers.' By May the Enforcement Council of the federal Wartime Prices and Trade Board had taken an interest in short service as a possible violation of price controls. The LCB informed federal authorities that it had 'no objections whatever to your organization prosecuting in any case where it is justified.'[41]

When the BCHA received this information, its president called a meeting of the member hotels from Vancouver and neighbouring municipalities. The meeting agreed that short service was 'the most serious situation that has ever confronted the hotelmen since beer by the glass was inaugurated.' The president claimed that rogue members would 'wreck the industry by serving a short glass of beer.' The BCHA then hired its own inspector to police the hotels. Its secretary reminded members that federal price regulators also had inspectors and that a conviction would bring not only a fine and jail sentence, but also 'an indefinite suspension of the license by the Liquor Control Board.'[42]

While the beer shortage was most severe in British Columbia, short service was not confined to the province. With liquor still rationed in 1946, the national association of liquor control boards agreed that the only solution was to mark each glass with a fill or load line. After 1 June 1946 BC parlours could use only glasses with what the Victoria *Colonist* dubbed a 'Plimsoll Line.' The eight-ounce glass was supposed to yield no less than 6.5 ounces of beer; in effect, a glass could contain almost 20 per cent foam. From a patron's point of view, the fill line had entrenched short service, as it usually marked the maximum rather than the minimum amount of beer in the glass. Not long after liquor rationing ended in 1947, the board allowed the parlours to dispense with load lines, at least for a while, but many kept them. The issue of short service never again acquired the intensity that it had during the war, but its practice remained one of the more common complaints against parlours.[43]

All those involved constructed short service in explicit gender and class terms. Many rank-and-file men may not have understood the theoretical implications of surplus value, but they knew when they were being cheated. Short service meant being short-changed. Yet short service was also linked to the war effort. Working men who were not at the front still took pride in their contribution. A full glass of beer was the entitlement of the productive working man who had 'done his bit,' even if he was not in uniform. A full glass was as much a qualitative as quantitative measurement, and war workers would not tolerate the implicit criticism that they could detect in beer foam. As well as invoking considerations of value and pride, beer foam also bubbled with class aesthetics. Although his specific example came from New York City, a representative of a Vancouver brewery told the BC attorney general after the war that wage workers wanted 'a full glass of beer without foam.' By contrast, a white-collar drinker 'likes to see a good head on his beer.' Those aesthetics, however, were not consistent. Local 676's handbook for 1950–1 recommended that tapmen follow the Plimsoll guidelines – that is, 'a desirable glass of draught beer should include about 20% foam.' Beer foam could divide workers as well as unite them.[44]

Local 676 was noticeably absent from the beer debates at the V&DLC – not surprising, since short service pitted parlour workers against workers as customers. Operators used explicit coercion against parlour workers to pull and serve short glasses. Yet workers also acquiesced in the practice because it could lengthen their paid workday. Casual workers were paid by the hour, and steady workers technically were guaranteed only four hours of work each day. When the beer ran out, parlours closed, as the delegates had noted at the Quebec City labour convention. For operators, four hours of operation coincided nicely, too nicely, with the 6:00 p.m. break for supper, which may partly explain why the board moved the closing time to 6:30 p.m. for Vancouver in May 1944.[45]

For the BCHA and the LCB, short service was as much about control as it was about beer. For political reasons the provincial government did not want the price to rise, and the LCB had to make sure that parlours did not break the rules. The board in turn placed the regulatory burden on the BCHA. Even with its own inspector and additional assistance from federal regulators, the hotel organization could not control recalcitrant members. Such an apparently simple issue as a full glass of beer turned out to be a significant site of regulatory contention.

Conclusion

Examining the inside world of workers and operators in BC beer parlours reveals an example of how class interacted with regulation. From the beginning, state officials assumed that beer parlours would be predominantly working-class institutions. Just as important, state officials defined them as such. Class informed state regulation, and official regulation attempted to reshape class. Yet parlour operators and workers assumed much of the responsibility for regulation. This process linked workers and operators in ways that included but transcended 'us' versus 'them.'

An obvious class relationship existed between the beer parlour union and the BCHA. At the same time, however, the union and the BCHA, like parlour workers and operators, were part of an intricate regulatory process that tied them to each other and to the state. On the one hand, the complexities of regulation existed within the context of capitalist relations. Those relations set real limits on regulation. Parlours ultimately existed to make a profit for their owners, and that priority was never far below the surface. Despite the emphasis on regulation, patrons were paying customers, not inmates or patients. On the other hand, parlour regulation was too flexible to be captured in simplistic notions of 'us' and 'them.' Those categories certainly existed, but their content varied with time and circumstances. Thus workers and operators, union and employers, were bound in a relationship grounded in class but linked to the demands of regulation.

In his analysis of the lives of a group of young working-class men in Thunder Bay, Ontario, Thomas Dunk argues that wage labour constructed their lives, but he concludes, 'There is no specific form of working-class ideology, politics or culture.' In fact, his 'boys' expressed culture through what he called 'non-class' discourses that masked class conflict: racism, sexism, and militant heterosexual masculinity. The boys knew that they held subordinate positions, and they resisted – in a ritualized manner, through their leisure activities. What began as popular critique ended up as a celebration of the immediate: 'The sole reward for their effort [was] often, to become further embedded in the world they were trying to escape.' Their rebellion, then, was largely ceremonial.[46]

In beer parlours, singing, fighting, and excessive drinking can be seen as a cultural expression of class – a ceremonial rebellion against the dominant order. More important, however, the burden of containing that rebellion fell on parlour operators and especially workers. Waiters were the front-line troops of regulation. They stopped the fights and suffered the bruises, the ripped clothes, and the consequences if they made the wrong decisions.

Yet some parlour workers themselves also rebelled against the dominant order. Casual workers in particular – those with both the most and the least to lose – offered a popular critique by drinking on the job. Such drinking defied the state, the operators, and the union. In the end, however, these workers were left with little more than hangovers.

From a regulatory perspective, drinking on the job was significant. For the executive of Local 676 it was a serious problem. The parlour operators wanted complete control over the hiring process, and employees' drinking strengthened the employers' case. The issue was not just whether drinking undermined effectiveness, but also that the union sent workers who did not obey the rules. In order to defend the hiring hall – a limited form of workers' control – the union disciplined its members. The local also asked the state for assistance in policing parlour workers. One of the justifications for this action was that hiring-hall policies forced the union to send out workers who were unfit. The union turned to the state to help the union regulate members so that the hiring hall could be maintained.

Despite their class antagonisms, parlour workers and hotel operators were not always overtly at odds. For example, illegal gambling, or bookmaking, was a risky business because of the priority that the state gave to suppressing it, but in some hotels it produced collaboration between operators and workers. Waiters garnered additional income, and operators, more customers.

Moreover, the operators' Second World War scheme to serve less than full glasses of beer could not have succeeded without at least the acquiescence of parlour workers. This practice of 'short' service angered patrons who believed that their customary right to a full glass had been denied. This dispute was sufficiently serious to attract the attention of the various labour councils at a time when they were trying to deal with the more pressing issues of the war. For the record the councils were careful to lay blame at the feet of governments and the hotels, but on a daily basis short service involved a conflict between customers and parlour workers.

Short service also highlights the limits and inconsistencies of state regulation. It was an unintended consequence of liquor rationing, which was both a federal and a provincial undertaking, but not a particularly well-coordinated one. The federal government reacted more to pressure from the drys, while the province was drawn to rationing because of the problem of too many people and not enough beer. Moreover, federal and provincial tax policies increased the cost of beer to the operators, but neither level of government was keen to see the retail price rise.

Individual operators responded with short service, and in turn the province pressed the BCHA to force its members to cease the practice. While not a creature of the state, the employers' organization often existed in a symbiotic relationship with it. Yet the BCHA's executive could not exert sufficient leadership with its recalcitrant members and finally moved towards more coercive measures. The provincial government encouraged it to do so, and the federal government did the same because short service circumvented national price controls. In the end short service diminished not so much because of specific actions to quell it, but because beer rationing ended soon after the war.

We can end with that war worker seated at the parlour table after his shift, furious because his glass has too much foam. He gives the waiter a piece of his mind and considers a fist. The operator has an eye on the till and on the door; no inspector so far. The tapman pours as he is told. Wary of turning his back to the angry patrons, the waiter knows that the tray of glasses is light, but if the beer lasts, then so will *his shift*.

To understand parlour regulation requires more than simple models of social control or constructions of working-class culture as resistance to the social relations of production. At the same time regulation did not negate those relations. In Vancouver's beer parlours, class still mattered.

Chapter Three

Ladies and Escorts: Regulating and Negotiating Gender and Sexuality

In May 1925, the chairman of British Columbia's Liquor Control Board (LCB) told a reporter that he had considered refusing service to women in the recently opened beer parlours, but, according to the journalist, 'this appeared unreasonable and ungallant to the fair sex.' In less than a month, however, official gallantry had given way to other concerns. In June the chairman sent a circular to all licence holders warning them of 'the frequenting of "Licensed Premises" by undesirable women, and the serious difficulties which their presence creates.' He added that licence holders 'must take the consequences of allowing such persons to be upon the premises.' In the May interview the chairman had said that his goal was to 'surround the [beer] traffic with such [a] decent environment that the least possible amount of drunkenness and economic loss may result.' To him, the presence of some women now compromised the decency of beer parlours.[1]

In order to highlight the complexities of class and regulation, the previous chapter emphasized operators and workers. Here, however, I give a lot of room to the patrons, for they played a particularly active role in the regulation of gender and sexuality, both as objects and as agents. This chapter deals with four main themes – the early attempt to exclude women from parlours, regulation of patrons through monitoring of venereal disease, construction of partitions to isolate unattached men from unattached women, and the limited space available for gays and lesbians.

State officials envisioned BC beer parlours as places where working people would be allowed to drink, provided that they behaved decently. The gendered aspects of decency stood out prominently because parlours immediately became sites of contention. While women expanded the boundaries of heterosocial leisure, their success was limited, as we see in the patterns of segregated drinking and in the naming of unescorted women as prostitutes. Official standards of sexuality differed for men and women, but they upheld or normalized heterosexuality. None the less, gays and lesbians managed to carve out some space for themselves.

Women's Exclusion

While the achievement of the vote during the First World War neither conferred real equality nor fundamentally altered dominant values, the lives of women did not remain static after the war. Educational opportunities improved, and many middle-class women joined their working-class counterparts in the labour market for a few years between school and marriage. After a day's work, single women in particular were able to enjoy leisure activities that were now both more commercial and more heterosocial in orientation. Men and women together went to dance halls, amusement parks, and most of all to the movies. As Carolyn Strange has emphasized, reformers were keenly concerned about the moral problem posed by employed single women, especially working-class women. They seemed too independent and too interested in both men and leisure. Reformers feared that commercialized leisure would lure them beyond their wages and into prostitution.[2]

They worried, too, that young women would drink in hotel beer parlours. In the spring of 1925 Quebec and Alberta were the only other provinces that permitted licensed public drinking. Quebec banned women outright from taverns (the equivalent to beer parlours), and Alberta kept them out of urban beer parlours. In British Columbia the only specific gender restriction was that a woman could not serve beer unless she held the licence. Yet operators could not allow 'persons of a notoriously bad character, or disorderly persons' to enter a beer parlour. This general restriction applied in particular to female prostitutes.[3]

Government officials and operators of parlours feared that the prohibitionists would use the presence of women to damn parlours as havens for prostitutes searching for clients. According to the Vancouver *Province*, operators feared 'the building up of a considerable prejudice against their refreshment rooms if women are not forbidden entrance.' Liberal Attorney General A.M. Manson shared some of their concern. He sought a legal opinion and was advised in May 1925 that 'there is nothing apparent in the law or otherwise to prohibit such a licensee from excluding from his premises any person or class of persons he may consider undesirable (e.g. women).' The LCB passed on this information to the hotels, and before the end of the month some parlours in Vancouver had posted signs saying that they would not serve women.[4]

In April 1926 the Vancouver East Presbytery of the new United Church of Canada sent observers to watch Vancouver parlours. According to them, in an hour one evening, 2,396 men and 284 women entered fifty-four beer parlours; on another evening, 766 men and 143 women entered five beer parlours in one hour. Despite the low numbers of women, the presbytery passed a resolution 'that we view with alarm the proportion of women patronizing the beer parlors ... and we believe that many of the young people of our city are being subjected unnecessarily to temptation in various forms.' At an anti-beer rally in July 1926, J.D. O'Connell (dubbed an 'ardent prohibitionist' by the *Province*) declared: 'The greatest danger was in the beer parlour, where women are permitted.' The *Province*, which supported parlours, also expressed concern about women: 'There is no doubt that the presence of women makes it more difficult to conduct beer parlors in a decent and orderly manner.' In order to preserve the decency of the facilities, the paper recommended that the government consider excluding women.[5]

Prodded by LCB officials, the British Columbia Hotels Association (BCHA) voted unanimously in late July 1926 to ban women from Vancouver beer parlours. President J.D. Pearson announced that 'many men objected to the presence of women' and that the prohibitionists had denounced parlours for admitting women. The parlours acted to remove 'this chief cause for criticism' because 'we have no desire to give the public offense.' He added: 'No doubt, many women patrons will not appreciate the move,' but he assured them that they could still buy beer at government liquor stores. The Vancouver *Sun* questioned the legality of banning women but still strongly supported the move. An editorial noted that 'whatever an odd woman here or there may say about it, public opinion and particularly that part of it contributed by women, is strongly averse to women frequenting beer parlors.'[6]

Initially, the prohibitionists were critical of the ban, but gender equality was not their primary concern. Speaking at a meeting of the Anti-Beer League in July, Reverend R.J. McIntyre, of the British Columbia Prohibition Association, said that the ban represented 'the deathbed repentance of the brewers.' He criticized it for violating the idea of equal rights. More important, he used the decency discourse against the parlours. He claimed that the ban meant that parlours were unfit for decent women, and they 'made a man, for the time being, unfit to associate with his own wife. It was an admission that beer lowered a man's power to distinguish between right and wrong, and weakened his resistance to temptation.' Beer parlours attracted 'women of the street' and 'men of like repute.' The solution was to ban the beer parlours, not 'decent' women.[7]

At the time the ban was announced, the drys were trying to force another vote on beer parlours in Vancouver. If they could close the parlours there, they believed that their cause eventually would be victorious across the province. That goal, more than concern about equal rights, motivated McIntyre's comments. Both drys and wets realized the importance of Vancouver in the beer parlour debate. Technically, the ban on women applied only in that city.[8]

On 16 August 1926 the *Sun* announced the opening of 'Eveless Beer Parlors' in Vancouver. The temptress had been removed. In theory, however, the ban against women was voluntary. As a 'gentlemen's agreement' among the parlour operators, it worked only so long as everyone agreed to abide by it. In May 1927 the Commercial Hotel began to serve women again. When the police arrived on 25 May, twenty-nine of the approximately one hundred patrons were women, and 'a number' of them were described as 'under the influence of liquor.' The LCB quickly suspended the operator's licence. The chairman claimed that the suspension was for serving inebriated male patrons, but he added: 'I am determined that persons of questionable character shall not frequent licensed premises, and it is not always possible to guard against this condition if women are permitted.' Still, by 1927 liquor officials had come to the conclusion that the ban was not legally enforceable. The LCB reached a compromise with the Commercial Hotel, which allowed beer service to women in a separate room watched over by a security guard. Other hotels soon followed suit. The government drafted legislation that would have formalized gender segregation with separate licences for the men's and the women's parlours but did not introduce it in the House.[9]

In public at least, women themselves had little to say about the ban and separate facilities. Particularly odd is the relative silence of the Vancouver Council of Women (VCW), the city's prominent federation of women's groups, which was affiliated to the National Council of Women of Canada. As a middle-class, maternal-feminist reform organization, the VCW had long been a supporter of prohibition and campaigned for its continuation.[10]

Even before the first liquor stores had opened in 1921, the VCW's executive passed a resolution that said that because it was 'engaged in promoting the general welfare of women and children ... we place ourselves on record as strongly opposed to the sale of wine and beer, either in bottles or by the glass, in the hotels and restaurants of Vancouver.' At a general meeting just before the beer plebiscite in June 1924, members endorsed a motion that claimed that beer sold by the glass 'would practically mean a return to the Bar with all the evils that attend and that it would increase the temptation for the young people.' For the VCW the real issue was the parlours themselves. From its perspective, their existence was a serious threat to women and children and thus an affront to decency. In the 1920s a good possibility still existed that the parlours could be eliminated – a goal more laudable for the VCW than the false gender equality of mixed drinking.[11]

Some women, however, openly opposed their exclusion from the parlours. Mrs T.D. Tattersall, who lived on Pacific Street in downtown Vancouver, had approved of 'beer-by-the-glass for women.' She said that the excuse that women had to be banned because of 'bad women' was 'the worst insult ever offered to the women of Vancouver.' She made an open appeal to the city's female population: 'Our vote is threatened; let every woman in Vancouver who appreciates her suffrage get ready to protect it. This is the thin edge of the wedge. Don't let it go farther.' Many anonymous women supported Tattersall by patronizing the Commercial Hotel and other beer parlours. Some were no longer willing to agree that public drinking was an acceptable activity for men only, and they challenged men on their own turf. Tattersall even implied that a beer parlour might be a more decent place than home for women to drink because 'a glass of beer served in public was preferable to a dozen bottles in the home.'[12]

Charles Hurt of Vernon sympathized with Tattersall. He reacted forcefully to an editorial in the *Province*. On the one hand, it admitted that women had equal rights with men and that they had been served in beer parlours, 'without offense to public morality, and with little disturbance of public decorum.' Yet, on the other hand, according to the paper, 'these things do not count. There has come to be an instinctive aversion in the public mind – it exists, so the hotelmen say, among many of the men who frequent beer halls – against the idea of women in these places.' Hurt countered that the hotels wanted to ban women because their presence curbed consumption. He believed that women inhibited the excesses of male camaraderie and promoted decency: 'Certainly there are many men who can not be happy unless they are telling or listening to lewd stories or punctuating their conversation with a series of oaths, and such men do, no doubt, find their liberty of action circumscribed by the presence of ladies in the parlor. Practically all men have a substratum of decency and culture in their make-up, but that is no reason for the exclusion of the people whose presence makes for decency.'[13]

For the time being, the issue of women in beer parlours faded from the public gaze. The drys were not able to obtain another plebiscite. In 1930 the LCB's chairman informed the Alberta Liquor Control Board that legally women were not barred from BC parlours but that 'many licensees particularly in large centres have voluntarily provided separate rooms for the service of women and women with male escorts in an endeavor to safeguard their licenses by minimizing the risks thereto offered by undesirable females.' The goal was to separate unattached men from unattached women. Many parlours simply provided a separate area in the main parlour for solo women and women with male escorts. A few let the two sexes openly drink together, while others continued to ban women.[14]

Venereal Disease

Beer parlours attracted official attention again when they became indirectly part of a provincial campaign to check venereal disease (VD) transmitted by prostitutes. As a result, during the Second World War, the province ordered parlours to erect partitions to separate unattached men from unescorted women.

At the end of the nineteenth century, concerns about VD had exacerbated some people's fears about 'deteriorating racial stock,' and the racism of some English-Canadian moral reformers was a mix of hereditary and environmental assumptions. Women – more precisely, the respectable mothers of the 'Anglo-Saxon' race – had to be protected from the ravages of VD, so that they could continue to produce superior offspring. Those fears gave additional incentive to the promoters of social purity, because most doctors believed that 'prostitutes constituted the principal reservoir of the disease.' Nearly everyone tended to blame prostitutes, rather than their customers, for spreading VD. Respectable women needed to be protected, but deviant ones needed to be regulated.[15]

VD had become a particularly public issue during the First World War. By 1915, nearly 30 per cent of the Canadian Expeditionary Force in Europe was infected, compared with 5 per cent of the British forces. VD accounted for 12 per cent of all non-combat sickness in the military. The Canadian army fought the scourge with early treatment centres, 'short arm parades' (visual inspection of the genitals), and lectures on health and 'continence.' The Canadian army urged the English authorities to imprison 'infected women' in order to keep them from the troops.[16]

On this side of the Atlantic, Ontario in 1918 passed legislation that required all infected men and women to obtain treatment, and the province made it a crime to infect another person knowingly. British Columbia passed similar legislation, the Venereal Diseases Suppression Act, in 1919. That year the federal government created a Department of Health, with one of its ten divisions devoted to control of VD. Ottawa allocated $200,000 to fight VD, with most of the money to go to the provinces on a shared-cost basis. To receive money the provinces had to open clinics that offered free treatment. British Columbia opened treatment centres in Vancouver and Victoria. Infected people from outlying areas had to travel to those cities to receive treatment.[17]

While health officials urged a more scientific approach to control VD, moral sentiments remained prominent. Authorities still targeted prostitutes and other 'loose women' as the agents of infection. For many doctors, VD remained a moral issue as well as a health problem. Some opposed free treatment, as they believed that the diseased should have to pay for their 'sins.' Most doctors would not endorse the use of condoms; the risk of disease was meant to encourage abstinence. As well, condoms were considered birth control devices and thus were illegal under the Criminal Code.[18]

In November 1936 the provincial secretary announced a new campaign to reduce VD, which he claimed affected 20 per cent of the population. The five-year plan, implemented beginning in 1937, called for more VD clinics, a public awareness program, and increased enforcement. According to Dr Donald H. Williams, who was appointed director of the Division of Venereal Disease

Control in the Provincial Board of Health in 1938, the key to eliminating VD was 'a policy of vigorous enforcement of law directed against commercialized prostitution.' Between October 1936 and August 1940 the board's Vancouver office examined sixty-five 'professional prostitutes' and found 70 per cent infected with gonorrhoea or syphilis or both.[19]

In February 1937, at the suggestion of the LCB's chairman, the secretary of the BCHA had sent a letter to all members warning them 'not to allow men unaccompanied by a lady, to be seated in the ladies' part of the beer parlour.' He added that 'if present conditions are not rectified at once,' the LCB might compel operators 'to put in a ceiling high partition definitely dividing the ladies' section from the men's.' The BCHA's secretary also pointed out that some operators had allowed some patrons 'to become very unladylike and ungentlemanly in their conduct.' He concluded by noting that 'present conditions' could put beer parlours 'into disrepute in the eyes of the public, thereby jeopardizing our franchise.'[20]

His concern was justified. In a January 1939 speech to the Vancouver Board of Trade, Dr Williams claimed that 'in many of the mixed beer parlors of Vancouver there is at least one prostitute who plies her trade in a room in the hotel to which the beer parlor is attached.' By the end of the month the chairman of the LCB had decided that 'in view of the publicity being given to the present vice-drive in the City of Vancouver,' the LCB would work even more closely with the Division of Venereal Disease Control. Patients of public health clinics who admitted that 'contact was made in a beer parlour or while under the influence of liquor' would have their liquor permits cancelled. While the ruling was technically gender neutral, the expectation was that the patients would be men who had been infected by women.[21]

Initially at least, the BCHA pledged its full cooperation with the Provincial Board of Health 'in connection with the problem of prostitution and VD.' In March 1939, however, Dr Williams informed the BCHA that, despite the crackdown, there were 'still a considerable number of known prostitutes and known infected patients using the beer parlours in Vancouver.' He added that 'the prostitute is the main root and source of VD in this province' and that tracking infected prostitutes often took health officials to beer parlours. Dr Williams was particularly concerned because he claimed that 'alcohol flares an almost healed gonorrhoea into full blown activity and it cancels out the value of treatment in syphilis.'[22]

By the autumn of 1939 the BCHA had become fed up with Dr Williams and his focus on parlours. In October its secretary wrote the private secretary of the federal minister of health in anticipation of a visit to Ottawa by Dr Williams. The BCHA claimed that he had 'hounded and harassed the beer parlors,' even though the unlicensed 'ten cent dance halls' constituted 'the main source of [venereal] pullution [sic].' The secretary added that Dr Williams had 'faked statistics' in order to discredit the parlours. He believed that the doctor's ultimate goal was to 'wreck the beer parlor business.'[23]

With the beginning of the Second World War, however, Dr Williams intensified his campaign, and the hotels had little choice but to cooperate officially. Dr Williams referred to beer parlours 'frequented by diseased women' as 'an alien fifth column which is insidiously undermining the health of His Majesty's Forces and spreading infection to potential recruiting material among the young male population.' In April 1942 he sent the BC attorney general a list of nineteen Vancouver beer parlours that he considered 'a menace to national defence' because of 'diseased prostitutes using their premises for solicitation.'[24]

Later that month the LCB and the BCHA agreed that facilities in Vancouver, Prince Rupert, and Esquimalt would erect barriers that would physically separate the area reserved only for men from that for 'ladies and their escorts.' They encouraged parlours elsewhere to raise such barriers. While the BCHA resented the harsh opinions of Dr Williams, the parlour operators knew that they had to be seen publicly to be taking action. Almost as soon as the war started, prohibitionists had launched a campaign to curtail public drinking for the duration, and by 1942 they had achieved some support. By mid-June the parlours had the partitions in place. In 1943 the Division of Venereal Disease Control changed its letterhead slogan from 'Prevent Prenatal Syphilis in Children – A Blood Test for Every Expectant Mother' to 'Venereal Disease – The "Master Saboteur" of War Effort.'[25]

Throughout the war, the division monitored cases of VD allegedly acquired in beer parlours. To track them, it relied almost exclusively on interviews with infected men. Official records imply that women transmitted VD to men: 'It has come to the attention of this Division that five male patients who are under care for acute gonorrhoea allegedly acquired their infections from girls, not previously known to them, whom they met in beer parlours in this city.' They do not state that at some point, of course, these women were probably infected by men. The documents implicitly assumed that single women who met men in beer parlours were prostitutes, or at least women of 'suspected promiscuous habits.' In one encounter at the Rainier Hotel on Carrall Street, a man invited 'a girl who was sitting alone' to join his group. The two went to his room, 'where the exposure occurred. No charge was made by the girl.'[26]

Despite official views, venereal infections allegedly acquired in beer parlours hardly constituted a threat to national defence. Between 1939 and 1944 the Division of Venereal Disease Control attributed 562 cases of VD to BC beer parlours. Of those, 513 were in Vancouver, and the Halfway House in Esquimalt on Vancouver Island accounted for nearly half of the rest. In 1939, before the war and the influx of military personnel to the province, Dr Williams reported that the Vancouver clinic alone treated 1,600 cases each week. In 1942 the military infection rate was less than half that of the civilian rate in Vancouver, and the Vancouver *News-Herald* said that the city 'boasts one of the lowest V.D. rates on the continent.'[27]

The complaints of the BCHA had at least some credibility, and liquor officials did not always side with their colleagues in the Provincial Board of Health. The LCB's chairman agreed with the BCHA that health officials relied too exclusively on interviews with infected men. As William Kennedy told the new director of the Division of Venereal Disease Control in 1944, 'If a patient is too drunk to remember where he was at the time the contact was made, it is hardly fair to accept his statement that it was in a Beer Parlor as it might just as easily have been in some other place.' While he pledged the LCB's continued cooperation, he also questioned the 'advisability of simply accepting the statement of a patient without anything else to back up the charge made.'[28]

Official concern about prostitution and VD continued after the Second World War. With the introduction of sulpha drugs in the late 1930s and penicillin in 1943, many people believed that VD would disappear. According to the Division of Venereal Disease Control, however, when British Columbia abandoned wartime liquor rationing in 1947, one result was an increase of venereal infections allegedly acquired in Vancouver beer parlours. In response, the LCB, hotels, and health officials created an informal 'facilitation' committee. Within a couple of years the membership had expanded to include the police, religious representatives, and social workers. The committee met quarterly to discuss ways to reduce contacts between prostitutes and potential clients in public places. The continuing battle against prostitution and VD may have had little effect on either, but it continued to broaden parlour regulation beyond the state.[29]

Yet state coercion remained a regulatory tool. In 1947 the government updated the 'Venereal Diseases Suppression Act' of 1919. Infected people now could be 'detained' for up to a year if they refused or did not continue their treatment for VD. In addition, 'as a means of improving the liaison between the City Police Department and the Health authorities,' a 'Police Station Examination Centre' was opened in Vancouver. 'Each morning all women in custody' were 'examined routinely for venereal disease.'[30]

Negotiating Decency

Analysing gender segregation and monitoring of VD reveals the values of the authorities and the ways in which they regulated parlours. Yet parlour partitions underscore the dynamism of regulation and the negotiation of decency that occurred within the parlours. Liquor and health authorities could not simply, on their own, decide what was appropriate behaviour in beer parlours, issue the decrees, and exercise sanctions.

From the beginning, parlours were considered morally compromised space frequented by morally suspect people. State officials both defined how such people should behave and tried to regulate space so that patrons had little choice but to act in the approved way. Partitions were a physical manifestation of these goals. Yet many patrons, men and women, resisted that discourse, and they influenced the direction of regulation – as we can see in the state's ever-more-stringent attempts to isolate unattached men from unattached women.

On a small scale, partitions preceded the Second World War. Encouraged by the LCB, in 1928 the Grand Union Hotel on Hastings Street set aside a small area with a partition four feet, six inches, high, which the inspector concluded was 'much better than allowing the few ladies that do patronise the premises to be sitting around indiscriminately with men.' A small sign, 'Ladies Parlor,' was suspended from the ceiling. Working with the LCB, the BCHA encouraged introduction of these partitions, and neither body was pleased in 1931 when Mr W.C., operator of the New Empire Hotel parlour, a couple of doors away from the Grand Union, reduced his partitions to three feet. The chief inspector concluded that low partitions were 'no help towards the decent conduct of the licensed premises. I have always insisted on said partitions being high enough to prevent conversation and ragging going on over them.' He told Mr C. that he wanted the partitions raised to four feet, nine inches, because 'we are having considerable trouble over the women question and everything is being done to obviate disorderliness.'[31]

By April 1942, when the board ordered all Vancouver parlours to install barriers, the partitions had to be a least six feet high and constructed to 'permit no visibility' between the two parlours. To facilitate beer service, one eight-foot wide opening was allowed, and on Saturday nights licensees could erect movable partitions to expand or shrink either parlour. Soon after the war the partition height was raised to six feet, nine inches, and a movable partition now required the approval of the board, with an explanation for its necessity.[32]

After the LCB received statutory authority to force hotels to improve their facilities, restrictions became more elaborate. Higher, more permanent partitions moved closer to the service bar, as one bar usually served both parlours. Of some parlours the LCB demanded a partition right to the bar or a gate between the partition and the bar. When simple swing gates failed to control patrons, the board asked for locked gates or those with electric devices to open and close them. The board also required that some parlours hire floormen to guard the gated area or the increasingly common separate street entrance for women and escorts.[33]

Still, LCB inspectors grew increasingly frustrated with their inability to check what they called 'crossovers' or 'wandering.' Crossing over most commonly involved unattached men entering the ladies and escorts' parlour or walking from the men-only to the mixed side. 'Wandering' referred also to movement within a beer parlour, particularly men moving from table to table on the mixed side. Inspectors claimed that some parlour operators did little to stop unauthorized movement.[34]

In March 1949 the West Hotel on Carrall Street had its licence suspended for male 'crossovers' that led to venereal infections. In July the BCHA had hired an observer on the West's behalf; he reported that a hired doorman turned away twenty-two men from the ladies' entrance on one day and thirty-three on another. In June 1951 an inspector described an unusual example of wandering in the New Fountain on Cordova Street: 'Two men – unattached – were observed carrying their table, full of beer, over to two un-attached females.' According to health authorities, one male venereal patient made good use of both the New Fountain and the nearby Stanley Hotel in 1953: 'During a ten day drinking and sexual spree ... he picked up six (6) women in these parlours, always walking directly into the women's entrance.'[35]

While the inspectors' files are full of references to male 'crossovers' and 'wanderers,' occasionally women took the initiative. In May 1949, for example, an undercover investigator in the

Royal Hotel on Granville Street noticed 'ladies in the mens [*sic*] section. One woman standing at the bar drinking beer.' From the agent's point of view their behaviour may have been brazen, but it was also brave. Men, properly accompanied, were expected to be on the ladies' side, but the men's side was completely closed to women. Obviously a woman stood out prominently on the men's side; just as important, many men wanted no women there. Others assumed that women who entered their side were making themselves sexually available. The inspector at the New Fountain in June 1951 watched an unescorted woman enter 'the Mens' section to see who was there.' To him her 'profession was obvious.' Unescorted women who wanted male company usually encouraged men to go to the ladies' side, where they could exert more control. A woman who received unwanted male attention on her side could have her harasser ejected as an unattached man.[36]

The most elaborate and most expensive restrictions that the LCB ordered were duplicate facilities. This process began with the requirement that a men's toilet be installed in the ladies' parlour. A common method of crossover was for a man to say, as he moved from the men's to ladies' side, that he had merely been on the men's side to use the toilet. By the 1950s the model hotel had separate street entrances for each parlour, with both doors identified, and a third entrance for the hotel lobby. A central bar had an unobstructed view of the entire parlour area. A men's toilet was located in the ladies' parlour, and each parlour had its own pay telephone, even if business did not warrant two phones.[37]

The official regulations, however, were not always the ones imposed. For some hotels, particularly the older, smaller ones, these new standards were difficult and expensive to achieve. The board's acceptance of deviations from the standards was often linked to patrons' behaviour. For example, from 1948 on, the inspectors noted that the Angelus Hotel on Dunsmuir Street had no men's toilet in the ladies' parlour. The inspectors were patient until 1954: as 'no complaints have been received regarding the operation of these premises it has not been found necessary to request the Licensees to bring it up to standard.' By contrast, the

New Empress Hotel on East Hastings did not appear to have sufficient frontage to provide separate entrances, but it had quite a problem with crossovers. The chief inspector in 1949 proposed that 'this is one of the premises where service to women should be disallowed.' It was not.[38]

Still, we should be wary of the inspectors' files. A parlour that caused little trouble warranted little attention or record keeping. Even temperance groups, which damned *all* parlours from the beginning, had to acknowledge during the initial intense debate over them that some parlours were quiet, orderly places. About 1930 (the document is undated), the British Columbia Temperance League compiled a list of what it called 'Beer Saloons in Vancouver and Record.' For many entries the compiler included a short description, such as 'A Dive' (the Dominion). Yet it described the Haddon as 'Decent' and three others – the Ivanhoe, Kingston, and Martinique – as 'Rather Decent,' and none was located in a first-class hotel.[39]

Moreover, the LCB used its coercive powers to encourage parlours to comply. It worked closely, if not always harmoniously, with police and health officials. It also had statutory authority to 'suspend or cancel any beer licence for such reason as to the Board may seem sufficient.' In addition, liquor authorities sent parlour operators lists of interdicted persons, who had lost their right to purchase liquor.[40]

With the full support of the LCB, parlour operators took the initiative to ban specific individuals who were considered troublemakers. More often than not, those banned were women accused of being prostitutes. After a visit from the LCB inspector in December 1947, the operator of the West Hotel 'barred 17 known prostitutes' and sent the list to the LCB. The list showed the compiler's familiarity with the women, identifying all but two only by their first name or a nickname, such as 'Shanghai Lil,' 'Big Betty,' and 'Irene,' the 'Logger's Queen.'[41]

These specific women may or may not have been prostitutes, but the LCB and parlour operators often named female drinkers as suspected prostitutes, which had real regulatory effect. After the December inspection of the West Hotel, the LCB sent an undercover investigator to watch the parlour. On 23 December 1947 he commented that 'no open soliciting was seen, but the women companions of the men patrons were rather of the easy virtue type.' On the 29th he still saw no soliciting, but 'some of the women present did not come under heading of "ladies."' On 11 January 1948 he again saw nothing untoward, but 'some of the women present looked as if their professions were more ancient than honorable.' Later that year the hotel banned all single women from registering as guests.[42]

The West Hotel was not unique. In 1948 the Europe Hotel on Powell Street also prevented single women from registering. After a 1952 warning from the LCB, the operator of the New Empire's parlour informed unescorted women that they could no longer sit near the front door of the ladies' parlour. They had to sit farther back, in full view of the tapman and waiters. In 1953 the LCB forwarded a complaint from the Division of Venereal Disease Control to the operator of the Main Hotel's parlour. The manager responded that 'we have been seeking recently to determine positively which of our female clients are questionable so that we may in the future keep a particular watch on them, refuse them service, or otherwise keep them away from our premises.' In March 1954 the operators of the Roger Hotel, formerly the Pennsylvania, informed the LCB that they had 'barred from the licensed premises all women who would appear to be of an undesirable character.'[43]

Not all the restrictions placed on women stemmed from assumptions about alleged illicit sexuality. Some were motivated by conceptions of women as primarily responsible for nurturing children. In 1949 the Department of National Health and Welfare asked that provincial-government liquor stores refuse to cash family allowance cheques. British Columbia's LCB went one step further and requested that all licensed premises refuse them: 'Anything you can do to prevent the cashing of these cheques in the premises under your control will be greatly appreciated.' These cheques were payable to mothers, not to fathers. We can infer that women supposedly needed more regulation, as they might drink beer at the expense of their children.[44]

Effective restrictions placed on male behaviour were less obvious. Parlour regulation circumscribed male sociability, but it certainly did not eliminate it. On the men-only side, small tables and the ban on standing while drinking usually prevented large gatherings, but in small groups men could still chat, boast, and treat each other to drinks. Treating remained the mainstay of beer purchase by men in groups. It reinforced male reciprocity, and opponents had long argued that it promoted excessive consumption, since a man would lose face if he left before he had bought his round.[45]

Even if treating per se did not encourage consumption, men were fairly free, and freer than women, to consume lots of cheap beer, and drinking capacity remained a marker of masculinity. Serving intoxicated people violated the rules, but intoxication was a subjective and gendered assessment. The real limits for men were excessive rowdiness, its opposite, sleeping, or loss of control over bodily functions. In September 1951 an undercover agent said that he saw a man 'so drunk that he urinated in his chair,' and 'he was allowed to stagger around' and then return to his chair. When he arose again, 'his posterior was soaking wet, plus the front of his trousers and a large pool had formed under his table.' The incident sparked a visit from an inspector. A waiter assured him that the man had been cut off because of his drunken condition, but he had not lost control of his bladder. Instead, opined the waiter, the man had carried a bottle of something that had somehow leaked, after which he was removed from the premises.[46]

The public expression of masculine sexuality was less restricted than women's. The authorities assumed that some men, given the opportunity, would seek the services of prostitutes. Obviously the LCB tried hard to prevent unaccompanied men from encountering unescorted women – with mixed results, at best. These efforts regulated women more than men and were directed to the ladies and escorts' side.

Gays and Lesbians

Ironically, the requirement of a men-only parlour facilitated the gathering of gay men. As David Churchill has noted for Toronto taverns, the attempts at strict regulation of heterosexual behaviour opened up possibilities for 'same sex sexuality' and 'helped to create a surprisingly rich and varied gay life during the 1950s.' In Vancouver, some parlours became gay sites, but not exclusively so. By the early 1950s the Castle Hotel on Granville Street was known as a gay rendezvous. While drinking with a group of men at the Castle, one character from Peter Trower's novel *Dead Man's Ticket* is shocked to learn that his friend, a fellow logger, is gay: 'It finally dawned on me that they were all faggots, including my supposedly straight-arrow partner ... You can bet I got right out of there in a hurry.'[47]

The New Fountain on Cordova Street was also known for its homosexual clientele. Yet the venue, in the heart of skid road, appealed to lesbians as well as to gays. Lesbians, because they were women, had less access than gay men to public spaces where they could feel comfortable and be free from harassment. The New Fountain would accept anyone's money, and Trower's fictional and heterosexual Terry Belshaw describes the patrons: 'The customers were mostly women, some of them in black leather jackets and ultra-short haircuts and making no secret of their sexual preference. I recognized Mitch the Witch with a smashing brunette. He acknowledged me with his decadent choir boy smirk. On tighter scrutiny, I saw that his seemingly-female companion was a man in drag.'[48]

Stephanie Ozard remembers cruising Granville Street in the late 1950s looking for a lesbian bar. An unsympathetic man told her that she belonged at the New Fountain. Despite the 'drunks and drug addicts,' she was pleased to find a meeting place for lesbians. There were three other parlours in the same block, but only the New Fountain was known for its lesbian and gay patrons.[49]

After the period under consideration here, the Main Hotel, on Main Street, became the Vanport Hotel and a gathering place for

Vancouver's lesbian community. Perhaps less rough than the New Fountain, the Vanport was still a tough, working-class beer parlour, but Ruth Christine remembers it fondly: 'It was a dive, but it was fun.' In the 1960s Leah Curtis patronized both parlours, but she preferred the New Fountain. As a black woman, she felt rejected by the predominantly white women of the Vanport, whom she described as 'mostly just uppity white people.' Continually in trouble with both city and liquor officials for reasons other than its lesbian clientele, the Vanport closed in the mid-1970s.[50]

The LCB did not appear to make the suppression of homosexual sociability a high priority. For example, it considered the New Fountain one of the more notorious beer parlours, but not because of its lesbians or gays. In 1951 an inspector submitted a long, detailed report on the wild conditions there over a three-week period in June. His antipathy was obvious: 'The worst I have seen during my service with the Board.' Yet his concerns were prosaic by beer parlour standards: drunkenness, crossovers, prostitutes, and incredible filth and stench.[51]

David Churchill has argued that liquor inspectors in post-1945 Toronto were aware of the presence of gay men in working-class taverns. Yet any anxiety they expressed about their patronage reflected their own personal feelings rather than any liquor board policy directed against gay men. The Ontario board seemed more interested in explicit violations of the liquor act.[52]

At least as far as gays in working-class facilities are concerned, Vancouver and Toronto appear to stand in contrast to New York state. George Chauncey has emphasized that with the end of prohibition in 1933 and the creation of the State Liquor Authority, officials in New York city were unrelenting with their campaign against even the presence of gay men in bars. Their efforts intensified after the war, despite a court ruling that the simple presence of gay men was not illegal. Elizabeth Kennedy and Madeline Davis make a similar argument about Buffalo, New York. The State Liquor Authority's harassment of gay and lesbian bars there in the late 1950s 'created a grim period for lesbian social life.' It seems fitting that the rebirth of the gay liberation movement – the Stonewall rebellion of June 1969 – began outside a bar in New York city.[53]

Still, one should be careful not to place too much emphasis on official toleration of homosexual sociability in Vancouver's beer parlours. In Canada during the Cold War, as in the United States, homosexuals were purged from the federal civil service, and opinion leaders reinforced strict gender roles based on the heterosexual family. At best, gay acceptance in Vancouver beer parlours was backhanded. Beer parlours were constructed as working-class centres of excess that needed constant regulation. The presence of gays and lesbians was just another example of parlour debauchery – one of the many with which busy officials had to deal.[54]

As an example – admittedly an ambiguous one – in June 1954 an inspector made a routine visit to the Waldorf Hotel on Hastings Street. While he was inspecting the men's rest room, a waiter and a customer, presumably another man, came in, entered a toilet cubicle, and began to drink from a bottle of whisky. The waiter was suspended for illegal drinking, which was the entire focus of the inspector's report. Drinking whisky in parlour rest rooms was not uncommon, so why did the two men go into the cubicle? One is also tempted to ask what the inspector might have discovered had he entered the room sometime after the two men went into the cubicle. Maybe just two men drinking; maybe more. Yet the inspector did not seem to wonder, except to note where the illegal consumption occurred. The illegal bottle was on his mind, and that was his priority.[55]

The evidence is also silent as to what extent any toleration was paid for by bribery or other forms of corruption. Line Chamberland notes that lesbian bars survived in Montreal in the 1950s because of their links to organized crime. Closer to Vancouver, the Garden of Allah was Seattle's first gay-owned gay bar and operated from 1946 to 1956. For the Garden, the post-war years were anything but tolerant, particularly in the McCarthy era. Yet because its owners paid off the police, it was relatively safe from raids. Corruption associated with Vancouver beer parlours, so alleged the press, was widespread after the war, but it was usually linked to licensing, gambling, prostitution, and illegal liquor sales. Since no Vancouver parlour had an exclusively gay clientele, it is unlikely that police or liquor inspectors were paid off just to ignore homosexuals. Any such payments were probably part of a larger package.[56]

Keep in mind also that the regulatory priority in parlours was the suppression of illicit heterosexuality and related issues. Inspectors were attuned to a variety of gestures and types of behaviour that brought men and women together. Some probably did not see or were fooled by the fluidity of gendered behaviour.

While a single woman entering a parlour often aroused suspicion, two women or a group of women might not, especially if they were femme rather than butch lesbians. Moreover, sometimes butch lesbians chose to pass as men, which Line Chamberland argues is a good example of 'juggling gender categories and thus selectively making visible or concealing lesbian existence depending on the circumstances.' Gender could be juggled other ways. Carol Ritchie Mackintosh gained access to the elegant King Edward Hotel in Toronto in the late 1940s escorted by a gay man. Once in, he went his way, and she socialized with other lesbians.[57]

Gay men could pass as straight but still be visible to other gay men with use of well-understood codes, probably including use of the word 'gay' itself. Detection was even more difficult vis-à-vis transgendered people, whose appearance, performance, or physical attributes defied any simple or fixed categories of 'male' or 'female.' They could make a mockery of the separate sections for men only and for ladies and escorts and added another dimension to the idea of crossing over.[58]

The inspectors also may have conflated 'prostitute' with 'lesbian.' Donna Penn has argued that in the Cold War United States, social 'experts' tried to make lesbians more visible and dangerous by linking them to prostitutes as examples of sexual degeneracy. In working-class cabarets in Montreal in the 1950s, lesbians were sometimes arrested. As Line Chamberland notes, however, they were rarely charged with gross indecency. Like prostitutes, they were often arrested for 'underage drinking, va-

grancy, or disorderly conduct,' and 'while in jail, lesbians under-
went the same medical exam as prostitutes.' In Vancouver the 'bad
character' and 'disorderly persons' regulations were undefined,
and they could have been used against just about anyone. Yet they
were confined primarily to women named as prostitutes.[59]

For gay men one must also distinguish between sociability and
sex. On the men-only side, the LCB tried to make sure that male
interaction remained non-sexual. For example, in July 1952 an
inspector responded to a complaint about a hole in the wall
between two toilets in the men's washroom of the Stratford Hotel
on Keefer Street. He interviewed the manager and the bartender,
who admitted that this was actually the second hole that they
had found. The inspector did not leave until a janitor had 'put a
metal sheet covering over hole.' He also warned the operators
that 'they must keep a sharp look out for anyone going in Gents
washroom for immoral purposes' and that he intended to notify
the police.[60]

As Steven Maynard has argued, 'Holes made in the partitions
of lavatory walls were evidence of the extent to which men who
sought sex with other men appropriated public spaces for their
own sexual uses.' The city of Vancouver had long been aware of
such spatial appropriation. Public toilets built in the 1920s had
attendants' rooms with large glass walls so that officials could
regulate the behaviour of patrons. In beer parlours inspectors
paid much attention to toilets. The annual inspection forms required that they comment on the existence and kind of male
facilities in the ladies' parlour and on the general cleanliness of
all toilets.[61]

Inspectors explicitly linked cleanliness with morality, or as
Mariana Valverde has emphasized, 'unclean bathrooms were
evaluated from the point of view of the moral atmosphere of the
establishment.' In his tour of the disdained New Fountain in
1951 the inspector went to some detail to describe the toilets. Of
the women's he said that it 'rather defies description ... the floor
was swimming in liquor, urine, dirt etc and odor was terriffic
[sic].' As for the Men's: 'Conditions in the Men's rest room was
worse if anything, someone having vomitted [sic] all over the

toilet bowl and floor ... I presume this mess was left for the Chinese janitor.'[62]

Words were also tied to moral cleanliness. Officials also took a dim view of what they described as 'obscene writing' on washroom walls. Unfortunately, they never described the words they saw, although one undercover agent noted in 1951 that the name of the attorney general 'now adornes [*sic*] the mens washroom walls' in the Dodson Hotel. In 1953 the acting director of licensing decreed that parlours had to label their washroom doors simply 'Men' and 'Women,' rather than 'Ladies' and 'Gents,' or other, cuter names such as 'Queens.' Such labels struck him as flippant and detracted from 'the dignity that should surround the privilege of licence.' His ruling, he said, would remain in effect 'until we are sure that the patrons are all ladies and gentlemen.'[63]

Gay men had some success in making parlour washrooms a gay site, but gays and lesbians also sought out less regulated places. Beer parlours were subject to both police observation and LCB surveillance, but Vancouver's unlicensed cabarets and clubs did not receive regular LCB inspection. Considering both the stigma attached to homosexuality and its illegality, beer parlours were not necessarily the most hospitable places to meet.[64]

Conclusion

From the day in 1925 when beer parlours opened their doors, gender was prominent in their regulation because some women wanted in. Other females believed that a parlour was no place for a woman, a view shared by many men – patrons, operators, workers, and officials. Yet, while quite important, the presence or absence of women is only part of the regulatory significance of gender and sexuality. Fairly narrow but familiar concepts of heterosexual propriety were key components of parlour decency, and state officials attempted to reinforce dominant norms about gender and sexuality. Rather than being imposed and resisted, however, the results of regulation were a product more of negotiation among a variety of regulatory actors.

Patrons often challenged the dominant discourse of decency, especially the separation of unattached men from unattached women. Their success can be measured by both the imaginative ways in which they side-stepped regulation and the state's ever-increasing physical and policy efforts to control them. Parlour partitions were both a material manifestation of decency's expectations and a monument to the undermining of them. The patrons' effective challenge can also be read from the continuation of venereal disease in beer parlours.

For women the results were mixed. Women expanded the boundaries of leisure but did not eliminate them. Parlour partitions revealed the gendered, spatial dimensions of decency. For women the partitions were walls. 'Female' and 'decent' were linked only on the ladies and escorts' side. Even there, decency was defined in narrow ways. Unattached women were often defined as or akin to prostitutes. As Michaela Freund notes, naming women prostitutes was a powerful political device designed to 'control and regulate their sexuality, and not merely the sale of self.' A woman who entered a beer parlour by herself risked being treated as a prostitute. In many cases women were discouraged from entering parlours at all. Some were simply barred. Despite the open door and the assumption that women, at least decent ones, curtailed male excesses, in many ways little had changed. Women, public drinking, and illicit sexuality remained intertwined.[65]

For men the partitions were more porous, as male leisure space embraced female space. Porous, however, did not mean invisible. On the ladies and escorts' side, appropriate male behaviour was tied to the company of women. On the men-only side, patrons were freer to practise variations of traditional public drinking rituals. Some men saw the partitions as protection as they tried to recreate saloon sociability as best they could in an institution that was designed to prevent it. Men's sexuality was also far less regulated than women's. Men were chastised but not condemned for illicit sex, as long as their actions remained heterosexual.[66]

Despite decency's emphasis on heterosexuality, gays, lesbians, and transgendered people managed to find some room in beer parlours. In some cases they had to act 'straight' in order to stay. While no parlour had an exclusively homosexual clientele, a few were tolerant of those who refused to conform to straight ways. Gay men appear to have had more freedom than lesbians did. More surprising, suppressing homosexual sociability did not seem to have a high priority for state officials, as long as that sociability remained discreet. Officials, however, did attempt to draw the line when it gave way to sex in parlour washrooms.

Of course, patrons do not make the whole story of the regulation of gender and sexuality. Temperance groups, their clout diminished, still tried to set the moral boundaries of public drinking. In the 1920s and again during the Second World War parlour operators and liquor officials used gender segregation to blunt criticism of the parlours by temperance forces. The daily press also had regulatory influence. Unlike the drys, however, the newspapers supported public drinking, but they were initially critical of the presence of women. Instead, they promoted 'Eveless' parlours – that is, for men only.

Parlour operators, both as individual licensees and as members of the BCHA, also had an impact. For example, they pushed out alleged prostitutes, but they did not push too hard. Prostitutes were an attraction for some customers, and they provided additional revenue for some hotels, which rented them rooms where they pursued their trade. Parlours and prostitutes had more of a symbiotic relationship than either the operators or the LCB ever would have admitted in public. Official policy dictated that parlour prostitution would not be tolerated, but the authorities did not have the political will and probably not the power to eliminate it. Instead they helped regulate it, particularly by monitoring VD.

By the 1930s public health officials had become more prominent than moral reformers in the anti-VD campaign. Yet, as Claude Quetel notes, 'Anti-venereal discourse was not merely medical but moral.' In British Columbia, medical regulation was as much moral as scientific. Health officials blamed female prostitutes for the spread of VD, and they put women who had sex with men in hotels in the same category as prostitutes. Michaela Freud has perceptively argued that in Vancouver 'the prostitute came to be seen as the cause of VD, and was constructed as the diseased body, at the same time that the definition of who was a prostitute was extended to a large number of young, single women.' Official figures showed that prostitution in beer parlours was not a serious problem during the Second World War, but health authorities supported the installation and perpetuation of partitions to separate single men from unattached women. Liquor and health officials were not always of the same mind as to the best way to control beer parlour infection. While not openly defiant, the BCHA also took issue with state health authorities over controlling VD.[67]

Regulation was a diffuse and dissonant process on the ground. State regulation was not consistent, and the state certainly was not the only regulator. Other groups had their own agendas, including the patrons themselves. Depending on the circumstances, men and women both resisted and acquiesced in the expectations of decency, and their actions influenced the direction and design of beer parlour regulation. At least the people discussed in this chapter were, overall, accepted if not welcomed in beer parlours. We turn now to those who were not wanted, for they too influenced the regulation of parlours.

Chapter Four

Appearance and Performance: Creating and Regulating the Unwanted

On 18 October 1952 a man and a woman entered the ladies and escorts' side of the Martin Hotel's beer parlour in Vancouver. At first the waiter ignored them, and then, according to the couple, told them that mixed-raced couples were not served. If they wanted to drink, she could stay on the ladies' side, and the man would be served on the men-only side. The couple left. Quite embarrassed, the woman wrote to the LCB and asked about the legality of the refusal of service. She added that, on his own, her 'Hindu' friend had been served without incident at the Vancouver, Georgia, and Belmont parlours. After finding out that the Martin Hotel had a house rule that mixed-race couples would not be served, the chief inspector informed the woman only that the operator had 'the right to refuse service to anybody he does not wish to serve.'[1]

As we saw above, beer parlours did not welcome everyone. They discouraged unattached women and barred some patrons. This chapter looks more closely at those who were unwanted, not all of whom were patrons. Some people, such as minors and status Indians, could have nothing to do with parlours. Others could not work in them or own them. This proscription applied to non-citizens in general and to Asians (including citizens) in particular. Some barriers were entrenched in law, while others, such as refusing to serve blacks or mixed-raced couples, were the result of unwritten practices of the Liquor Control Board (LCB) or parlours themselves.

Yet to understand the unwanted requires us to go beyond rules and policies. The unwanted were real people, but they also fitted into official categories of concern. Because of the importance of appearance and behaviour, these categories were quite flexible. For example, an Indian was not always an Indian. A First Nations person could pass as white or, just as important, be accepted as one if his behaviour and appearance were appropriate. A banned mixed-race couple was a man of colour with a white woman. If the same man returned with an Aboriginal woman, the mixed couple ceased to exist.

Without a doubt the unwanted were often enmeshed in racial and ethnic discrimination. Yet, despite the long history of racial tension in British Columbia, race and ethnicity appeared to be small considerations in the regulation of beer parlours. Provincial state regulation was almost racially invisible, deceptively so. As the Martin Hotel example above shows, however, racial regulation was not far below the surface.

Beer parlour decency was quite racialized, but 'race' was sometimes, paradoxically, difficult to see because of its behavioural qualities. As Elaine Ginsberg has argued, 'cultural logic' has emphasized a biological foundation to race that shows in physical appearance. Yet racial categories are also performative – that is, people can also be defined in racial terms by their behaviour. People can be accepted as part of the dominant group if their behaviour is deemed appropriate to the circumstances. 'Passing' refers to how people change their identities and 'pass' as another race based on appearance, performance, or both. While passing can help explain how a variety of identities are constructed and shed, its historical origins are tied to race. Passing is usually associated with the 'desire to shed the identity of an oppressed group to gain access to social and economic opportunities.'[2]

In beer parlours, racialized behaviour had significant gender implications. Mixed-race couples became targets of regulation even though no formal rules excluded them. The reaction that they provoked emphasized the racial norms of decency. A man of colour 'racialized' himself – that is, engaged in indecent behaviour – if he was in the company of a white woman. Yet the woman also became less white, or pure, because of her behaviour. The potential for miscegenation threatened the dominance of white men and ultimately destabilized the category of 'white.'

Regulation was also linked to ethnicity. The seemingly innocuous category 'Nationality' on the annual 'Inspector's Hotel Report' is a good example. Directors and managers had to list their nationality, but this referred as much to origins as to citizenship. The simple title 'Canadian' was confined to those of white, Anglo-Celtic heritage. In a handful of instances the qualifier 'Jewish extraction' or 'Hebrew' was added to 'Canadian.' Some of the names were of eastern and southern European origin. In late 1940s an anonymous and disgruntled hotel operator asked: 'How do all these Greeks and Dagoes obtain licences?' His own response was that such undesirable people could obtain licences only through corrupt means.[3]

To work in or own a parlour one had to be a citizen. State expectations of parlour workers and operators were much higher than those of patrons because the potential for undermining state regulation was more pronounced with parlour workers and operators. The requirement was also a less-than-subtle method to keep Asians out of the business. Asians, notably the Chinese, were barred because of their alleged historic links with vice, particularly gambling and drugs. Their behaviour coupled to their appearance marked them as indecent and unwanted.

One did not have to be a citizen to drink in a beer parlour, but a patron did have to be an adult. The drinking age – twenty-one – was the same as the age of majority, or voting age. These restrictions linked minors with status Indians. Both were barred from beer parlours, although, as with Aboriginal people, some young people successfully passed as adults. Unlike minors, however, Aboriginal people had no guarantee that they would mature and acquire the rights of citizens, despite the state's policies of enfranchisement and assimilation. Even after beer parlours became open to them in 1951, equal access to alcohol continued to elude them for another decade. For many Aboriginal people, even if they did not drink, lack of equal access was a potent symbol of discrimination.

As with other aspects of parlour regulation, we see in this

chapter that dealing with the unwanted – be they mixed-race couples, Asian Canadians, minors, or Aboriginal Canadians – was not a linear process dominated by the state. In regulating Native people, legal authority was divided between federal and provincial officials, and they did not act consistently or even in harmony. Moreover, the unwanted were not simply acted upon. They also acted and influenced the process of regulation. Operators and other patrons also had regulatory impact, especially when race intersected with gender.

Race and Gender: Mixed-Race Couples

In 1938 Mrs Rose Low, operator of the Clarence Hotel's beer parlour, ordered her waiter not to serve Edward Rogers, a mixed-race man described as a 'Negro.' The LCB implicitly supported Low by not taking any action against the parlour. Rogers sued, and in court Low claimed that black customers had caused trouble in her previous parlour. Apparently, however, Rogers had caused no trouble and had been denied service simply because of his racial appearance. In 1940 the BC Supreme Court in this case ruled that a parlour could not discriminate on the basis of race. Low appealed, and in a split decision the Court of Appeal decided that freedom of commerce entitled her to discriminate against whom she chose. A minority report, however, argued that the refusal to serve Rogers 'because of his colour and race is contrary to the common law, [which is] founded upon the equality of all British subjects before the law.'[4]

The most explicitly negative racial comments in the records are about black men. When H.Y. complained about the Martin Hotel's refusal to serve her and her 'Hindu' companion, she pointed out that 'after all a Hindu is a British subject and not a negro.' With black men, race intersected with class. H.Y. was careful to stress that her partner was a businessman engaged in both the lumber and the petroleum industries. Black men in beer parlours were likely to be wage workers, often railway employees. In a complaint of January 1946 against the St Helen's for refusal of service to a black man, his white colleague, who lived in Ontario, stressed that they regularly travelled 'every province from Halifax to Vancouver.' A black man who was refused service with his white wife at the Regent sent his complaint on letterhead of the 'Brotherhood of Sleeping Car Porters.'[5]

Both the Canadian National Railways (CNR) and Canadian Pacific Railway (CPR) had stations in Vancouver's beer parlour district, and the CNR was Canada's largest employer of black men. In fact, Vancouver's small black community lived only a short distance from the CNR station, in an area popularly known as Hogan's Alley. As elsewhere, black people in Vancouver faced much racial discrimination. While a number of beer parlours had black patrons, blacks tended to frequent parlours in their own neighbourhood, especially the Stratford and Main hotels.[6]

Still, one should be careful about drawing too general conclusions. In the 1940 case against the Clarence Hotel, the plaintiff was a black shoemaker, not a railway worker. More important, the BC Supreme Court justice who originally ruled against the hotel spoke of the 'honesty, intelligence and kindness' of black railway workers and the need to 'consider their rights and the rights of their colored brethren with the greatest care.' This justice had more sympathy for black men than his colleagues on the Court of Appeal or at the LCB.[7]

After the Second World War some beer parlours continued to discriminate against black patrons, and some hotels would not rent rooms to them. In August 1948, for example, Charles Ross, a member of the United Packinghouse Workers, filed a union complaint after he was refused service in an unnamed beer parlour. He claimed that racial discrimination shortened the lives of black people by ten years.[8]

Yet the LCB's support for exclusion of customers based primarily on racial appearance diminished after the war, as official, open racism became less acceptable. In the example cited above, the refusal of service to a black man in the St Helen's parlour in 1946, his white colleague complained to the LCB. The board's secretary asked the operator on what grounds he discriminated against the customer. He also requested that the chief inspector look into the matter. The parlour operator soon apologized for the discrimination. He added that the waiter responsible was a spare who did not know that the parlour did not 'discriminate against serving coloured people.'[9]

More typically after the war, official concern was more directed at the behaviour of customers of colour. In 1953 an inspector lamented the problems in the Main Hotel caused by, he argued, the mixing of racial groups that drank too much. He described the customers as the 'most trying clientele in the city' and not 'a very pleasing sight.' Yet he did not know what could be done because 'if the hotel cracked down on the matter there is no doubt they would be accused of racial discrimination etc.'[10]

The LCB, among others, showed the least tolerance when men of colour accompanied white women. In two cases of alleged racial discrimination in the early 1950s, one at the American Hotel and the other at the Martin, the chief inspector had no hesitation in referring to the Court of Appeal's 1940 decision as justification for refusing service. In the American Hotel example he even went as far as to provide a complete citation for the case. There a waiter had refused to serve a party that included three white men, one Chinese man, and a white woman. An inspector interviewed the operator who told him that the hotel had a house rule 'that no mixed couples were to be served.' At the Martin Hotel, customers had helped to decide that mixed-race couples were not acceptable. According to the inspector, 'serving beer to mixed couples generally draws comment from surrounding tables which leads to trouble.'[11]

While the decision to exclude mixed-race couples appeared to be in the hands of the operators and customers, the LCB closely watched those parlours that did not ban them. In 1950 an undercover agent at the Stratford, which had a mixed-race clientele, 'noticed women patrons calling negroes into the ladies section ... The hotel seems to have a large number of white women who cater to this type of trade.' The incident sparked a warning letter to the operator, ostensibly for allowing crossovers, but constructed racially: 'Certain women patrons of your licensed premises were calling unaccompanied negroes into the ladies' section.' At the Main Hotel in 1951 an undercover agent 'noticed a group of negroes and white women' and was distressed to hear remarks like 'Lift them higher' and 'You can't put a square peg in a round hole' amid very loud 'shouting and laughter.' Shouting and laughter were not necessarily violations, but the chief inspector ordered an inspector to the hotel. The official concluded that the parlour complied with regulations. The unstated violation was the racialized behaviour of men of colour with white women.[12]

The records and the parlours defined 'mixed-race couple' narrowly. A mixed couple was a white woman with a man of colour, especially a black man. As categories of official and popular concern, women of colour with white men and mixed-race couples that included no white member simply did not exist. As real people, however, these couples drank in beer parlours. In particular, Aboriginal women were often linked with white men and sometimes with non-Native men of colour. Little emphasis was placed on the racialized coupling in these relationships. Instead Aboriginal women with non-Native men were usually dismissed as prostitutes or concubines.[13]

Virtually all liquor officials, parlour operators, and the majority of customers were white men. The explicit concern about mixed couples in which white women were participants and the disregard of those in which they were not underscored the privileging of white, heterosexual men. All women had the potential to be regulated by being named as prostitutes. Yet the threat to a racialized patriarchy was the mixing of white women with men of colour, hence the concern with the narrowly defined mixed-race couple. In the company of black men, white women racialized themselves – that is, they threatened the purity of their race.

Creating and Erasing Asians

Asians, especially the relatively large population of Chinese, stood out prominently in Vancouver. Popular and official assumptions about the impossibility and undesirability of Asian assimilation translated into policies of exclusion from the dominant society and concentration, both geographically in segregated areas and occupationally in menial jobs. Yet it was their alleged behaviour, the historic association with gambling and drugs, that racialized them in Vancouver beer parlours. Their exclusion from important jobs in parlours reinforced the policy of promoting decency.[14]

Asian exclusion in parlour regulation seemed non-existent. Yet the original regulations of 1925 required a parlour licensee to be 'a person who is registered or entitled to be registered as a voter in some electoral district of the Province.' This requirement was quite racial. Since Asians were denied the provincial franchise until after the Second World War, they could not obtain licences. When Mary Rosen applied for her beer licence for the Stratford Hotel in 1948, she was not registered to vote but was eligible, she said, because she was 'over 21 years of age, residing for more than six months, not Orientals [sic].'[15]

The Chinese received the provincial franchise in 1947, but that did not qualify them to obtain beer licences. In January 1952 the lawyer for a Mr P.C. asked the chief inspector 'of the policy of the Board as to Canadian born Chinese holding the licence of a beer parlour?' The next day the chief inspector replied that 'an application from a Chinese is not favourably looked upon by the Board as it has been found ... that Chinese are not able to handle this type of business.' The loss of the franchise cover forced the board to be more racially specific. Despite legal eligibility for licences, Chinese would not be allowed to compromise parlour decency.[16]

Official exclusion extended to working in parlours. Printed on every annual beer licence was the warning: 'No person shall be employed in any service in connection with the sale, handling, or serving of beer in, on, or about the premises in respect of which this licence is granted, unless he is registered or entitled to be registered as a voter in some electoral district of the Province.' The citizenship restriction thus eliminated Asians as parlour waiters and tapmen. Even after Asians received the vote, obvious Asian surnames did not appear on the list of parlour employees. Local 676 had never shown any interest in organizing them, and the union was consistently silent on the issue.[17]

Yet regulating Asians was more dynamic than racialized citizenship requirements. Despite exclusion, Asians, again particularly Chinese, worked around and in beer parlours. In 1944 the LCB's chairman informed Reverend R.J. McIntyre that 'Orientals' operating hotel rooms was a practice 'followed for a great number of years' but beyond the jurisdiction of the board. After the war two hotels, the Lotus and the Main, had Chinese owners. Both also had Chinese room managers, as did the Broadway, New Empire, and Pacific hotels. The Travellers Hotel had a Japanese room manager in 1954. At the New Empire in 1952 an inspector thought it important enough to note that the Chinese room manager 'supervises the clerks, who are white persons.' Finally, between 1947 and 1954 at least 15 beer parlours in Vancouver employed Chinese as janitors.[18]

The Chinese permeated parlour regulation in other ways. Like non-Asians, they sometimes worked in the illegal liquor trade that was linked to hotels. In 1948 the chief inspector informed the Vancouver police chief that 'in many hotels the clerks form a syndicate to supply liquor to hotel guests without the knowledge of the [beer parlour] licensee.' Neither the police nor the LCB appeared able to stop the bootlegging. In 1953 the 'Chinese operators of the rooms in the Lotus Hotel' pleaded guilty to 'keeping liquor for sale.' An inspector told the chief inspector that 'bootlegging at the above hotel has been carried on for some considerable time,' and he had informed the police. The chief inspector's response was to scribble an assurance to the chairman of the LCB that the beer licence was 'held by Occidentals, not Chinese.' Chinese vice may have compromised the hotel, but not yet the decency of the parlour.[19]

As we saw in chapter 2, the LCB took a noticeably firm approach to regulating illegal gambling or bookmaking, and race probably provided at least a subtext for that firmness. British Columbia had long constructed the Chinese as being a moral threat as habitual gamblers. The worst offender among parlours – the Lotus Hotel – bordered Chinatown, and Chinese owned the building and operated the hotel rooms. Yet Vancouverites of Chinese origin tended to gamble in their own establishments, not in beer parlours. In 1951, for example, the BC attorney general refused a club licence for the Chinese Democratic Society because, in his opinion, it would exist to 'enable gambling to take place.' Moreover, while many of the references to parlour bookmakers are neutral in regard to race (and gender), any surnames mentioned are non-Asian. Still, the historic link to gambling marked the Chinese as a threat to parlour decency and a reason to exclude them from operations.[20]

While the LCB prevented Asian Vancouverites from obtaining beer licences, it made no official effort to prevent them from drinking in beer parlours. Asians, however, do not appear to have been a significant presence. Inspectors often generalized about the class composition of patrons, and occasionally they commented on the racial mix of certain parlours. No parlour stood out as one that attracted a predominantly Asian clientele. After the Second World War – the only period for which consistent records exist – Vancouver's Japanese were still dealing with the aftermath of the forced diaspora of the removal of all Japanese from the west coast, seizure of their property and goods, and internment. While the Chinese preferred the nearby haunts of Chinatown, they did at least occasionally drink in beer parlours. For example, in a fracas at the Stanley in 1951 that involved a dispute between a white couple and the parlour's doorman, an inspector noted that the couple had been drinking with a male Chinese friend, who did not appear to be part of the dispute. Chinese men occasionally appeared more prominently as part of mixed-race couples, which, as we saw above, attracted a great deal of popular and official attention.[21]

Regulating Minors

As Mariana Valverde has noted, general prohibition gave way to 'a mad proliferation' of specific prohibitions. Beer parlours were notable sites of such rules, which excluded food, music, whisky, and the infamous stand-up bar from premises. Some bars dealt with people, and the most legally rigid applied to minors and Aboriginal people. Statutes denied both groups access to alcohol.

Inspectors warned operators to be on constant watch for minors and Indians. Legal paternalism assumed their inability to make responsible choices about alcohol. Chronologically at least, minors would grow up, but it was not clear when Aboriginal people could shed their dependent status. Moreover, and most significant, who was a minor and who was an Indian rested as much on performance, appearance, and subjective assessments as on legal definitions.[22]

The ban against minors in beer parlours was neither new nor remarkable. Even before prohibition, saloons had been off limits to young people. Temperance rhetoric had often invoked the dangers, direct and indirect, that alcohol held for children. When government control began, people under twenty-one were denied liquor permits and discouraged from even setting foot in a liquor store. During the debate over the return of licensed public drinking, the dry forces invoked the danger that beer would pose for children. One advertisement of 1924 pleaded for the electors to vote against beer 'for the protection of the boys and girls and the homes of B.C.' Major R.J. Burde, an Independent MLA from Vancouver Island, scoffed at that assertion. He claimed that minors were in more danger from the existing system because they illegally acquired liquor to take to unlicensed dance halls: 'The boys carry a mickey on the hip and the young flappers of 16 drink out of them.' Strict enforcement would deny minors access to beer parlours.[23]

On paper at least the restrictions about minors were prominent. The official regulations barred parlours from employing minors in any capacity. They obligated the operator to remove 'forthwith' any minor found on the premises. Even stricter were the statutory provisions against serving minors. When the parlours opened in 1925, the minimum fine for anyone supplying liquor to a minor jumped from $50 to $300 – a hefty sum in the mid-1920s. A subsequent conviction required imprisonment at hard labour for at least six months. At the discretion of the board, the operator's licence also could be suspended, but the burden of regulating minors fell primarily on parlour workers.[24]

Assessing the popularity of parlours with minors is impossible because young people who passed as adults would not be noticed, or perhaps not acknowledged, by the waiters or recorded in state records. The available evidence suggests that minors showed some interest in parlours. The number of prosecutions for providing liquor to minors increased after parlours opened their doors, but, more important, the law soon went after minors themselves. Other than the embarrassment of being tossed out forthwith, initially minors had faced no legal penalties for entering a beer parlour. After 1927, however, minors found in beer parlours were subject to the same $300 fine as the waiters who served them.[25]

Hefty fines, however, could backfire, as they did in one notable case in the Great Depression. In late 1932 the Vancouver *Province* reported that two Kamloops boys took two girls to a beer parlour in Chase. They got caught, and the boys were fined $300 each, or the alternative of three months in jail. Neither the boys nor their parents could pay, and one was supporting his widowed mother. The provincial attorney general intervened and reduced the fine to $50, but even that sum was too great. Determined that the boys endure some punishment, he said that he would remit both fine and jail if the boys agreed to be spanked by their parents 'in the place provided by Nature' under police supervision. The proposal was acceptable, at least to the parents.[26]

While the attorney general gets much attention in the newspaper account, the two girls are mentioned just once. We do not know if they were in the parlour or even if they were minors. Certainly no proposal was made to spank them. How the story was framed says much about the assumptions as to what motivated young males to enter beer parlours. The reporter noted that youths thought it 'smart' to drink in beer parlours. To pass made them 'heroes ... among their friends.' Thus the appropriateness of the punishment. The spanking was meant not to hurt them but to humiliate them for prematurely overstepping the boundary from youth to manhood. Spanking, an uncomfortable symbol of childhood, put them back in their proper place.[27]

A slightly different account of the same incident appeared in the Victoria *Daily Colonist*. According to it, four boys and only one girl were involved. All were described as under nineteen, and the reporter made it quite clear that the boys were indeed spanked by their parents. The girl was not spanked, but she did not appear to have entered the parlour. Despite these differences, the message was similar. The account uses 'youth' and 'boys' interchangeably. The transgressions are young male ones, and the explanation for their crime was 'that boyish big-feeling which associates adventure with entry on forbidden ground.' Again the emphasis is on keeping boys in their place. 'No youth,' the newspaper said, would 'boast about being turned upside down and paddled in the presence of others.'[28]

In his call for the return of licensed public drinking, Major Burde had asserted that beer parlours would allow men 'to drink like men in the open [rather than] make swillpails of their hotel bedrooms.' As Madelon Powers notes in her study of saloons, those institutions attracted boys because 'they were eager to learn how men were suppose to behave.' She notes that saloons often made some space for boys who might be there to sell newspapers or get beer for their parents. Beer parlours, however, provided no space for minors, which made the stakes higher. To pass as an adult might give a youth a head start on manhood and make him a hero to his friends. Yet, if he was caught, his treatment by his elders was often cool and firm. Manhood had to be acquired, to be earned, and queue-jumping minors deserved to be spanked.[29]

This view of minors and manhood has some merit, but it ignores the presence of female minors in beer parlours, and some young women were found there. Often they were in the company of young men. The Cecil Hotel, for example, was nearly directly across from the unlicensed Howden dance hall on Granville Street. One Saturday evening in December 1947 an undercover agent sat in the Cecil for over three hours. 'Couples, single women and single men' continuously slipped in from the Howden, and some appeared to be under age. The agent claimed that two workers did not ask for identification, and in fact both men attempted to 'kiss some of the women present.' In another case, however, an eighteen-year-old female was caught by herself in the Main Hotel. She had used someone else's adoption papers to deceive the waiter, but the documents did not fool the police. The waiter was not fined, however, because the police concluded that, because of the young woman's height, weight, and 'build,' she 'could possibly be taken for over 21 years of age.'[30]

While a few parlours appeared to tolerate minors, most took their exclusion seriously. Operators posted signs warning minors of the potential $300 fine. If a suspected minor could not produce adequate identification, he or she was refused service and told to leave. Alternatively an alleged minor could fill out a witnessed form that certified that he was an adult. It would seem that operators and waiters would have had much incentive to make use of these forms, which, with the stroke of a pen, transformed a minor into an adult. Yet workers still could be held responsible for those who neither looked nor acted like an adult, no matter what they had signed. These assessments were both subjective and flexible. A minor who worked hard to appear twenty-one before a waiter might later look quite different before a judge.[31]

Parlour workers were upset when, in 1947, the government lowered the fine for minors to a maximum of $50 while keeping the minimum fine for serving minors at $300. While the government reduced the financial burden on minors, or often their parents, what constituted a minor became more elastic. The prohibition against minors in beer parlours was broadened to include those 'apparently under the age of twenty-one.' Thus, a particularly young-looking legal adult could be transformed into a minor by entering a beer parlour.[32]

The expanded definition of minor gave little solace to parlour workers, who resented what they saw as the unfairness of the new provisions. In October 1948, G.A., a waiter at the Burrard Hotel, was fined $300 for serving a minor, and the parlour licence was suspended. The minor was fined $25. From a waiter's point of view, such minors engaged in intentional acts of law-breaking and deception but got fines much less than the busy waiter, who, in good faith, made an honest mistake. Members of the parlour

Stanley Hotel saloon in 1914.

Installation of a new bar at the Winters Hotel in 1914. Note the footrail, mirrors, and carved nudes.

Hotel Canada (later Marble Arch) beer parlour, c. 1925–6. While the parlour is crowded, the patrons are overwhelmingly male. Note the salt shakers; salted beer was quite popular.

Martinique Hotel beer parlour on Granville Street, c. 1930. George 'Monty' Rose, parlour operator, is on the left. Note the simplicity of the service counter compared with the Winters Hotel bar.

Clarence Hotel beer parlour, October 1939. The woman is probably Mrs Rose Low, who ordered her waiter to refuse service to Mr Edward Rogers, a mixed-race man (see page 82).

The interior of the upscale Georgia Hotel beer parlour, January 1935.

The interior of the fairly plain Regent Hotel beer parlour, 1940.

The interior of the Abbotsford Hotel beer parlour, April 1933. Note the hunting trophies and the booths on the right. The Liquor Control Board discouraged booths, but some parlours kept them.

Men and women drinking together in the Ambassador Hotel beer parlour, 1939. This area may have been reserved for ladies and escorts before partitions were required.

The infamous Stanley Hotel in 1940. It already had separate entrances for men and women. The New Fountain, equally infamous, is just visible to the left.

Unidentified men behind the service bar at the Dodson Hotel. Date unknown.

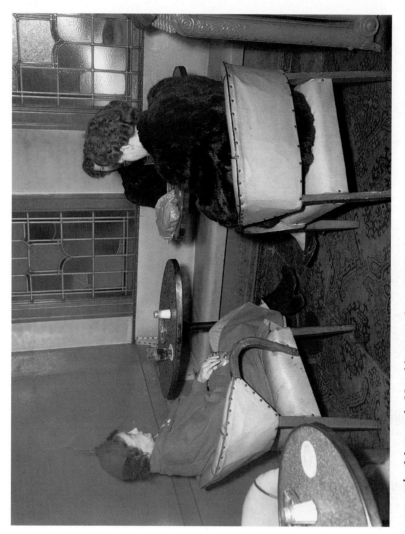

Female patrons at the Metropole Hotel beer parlour, 1951.

The unlicensed Palomar Supper Club could provide entertainment such as these dancers in 1950. Patrons illegally brought their own liquor to this and other bottle clubs.

Dal Richards, on saxophone, entertained at the Hotel Vancouver's swank Panorama Room, which was also a bottle club. This photograph was taken in 1950, but Richards was still performing in 2000.

A staged photo taken in August 1954, soon after the opening of the Russell Hotel cocktail lounge in New Westminster, near Vancouver. The bar had returned, but now with stools.

In 2000 the Empress Hotel on Hastings Street still had neon signs noting the former separate entrances for men and women.

union flooded the government with requests to reduce their legal liability.[33]

Their pleas fell on deaf ears. The new Government Liquor Act of 1953 retained the hefty fine for serving minors, while minors themselves were still subject to a maximum fine of $50. Moreover, young-looking adults now could enter beer parlours, but parlour workers were subject to a $300 fine for serving a person who was 'apparently under the age of twenty-one years.' As well, it would be up to a magistrate to decide what 'apparently' meant, based on 'appearance' and 'other relevant circumstances.' Thus what constituted a minor went far beyond age or documentation. 'Minor' was a malleable status, often defined by appearance, behaviour, and subjective assessments by waiters, police, and judges. Many years later, the president of the Beverage Dispensers Union dismissed the section of the Liquor Act on apparent minors: 'This terminology in legal application and practice, amounts to nothing more than phraseology.' Yet it was phraseology that had a real impact on the people involved, especially parlour workers.[34]

Making and Unmaking the Beer Parlour Indian

The conceptual tie between alcohol and First Nations has a long history in North America that dates back to at least the seventeenth century. The link is best encapsulated in what Joy Leland called the 'firewater myth' – the belief that Aboriginal people were 'more constitutionally prone to develop an inordinate craving for liquor and to lose control over their behavior when they drink.' This myth was powerful because Europeans used it to construct various images of the 'Indian.'[35]

In a study of Natives and alcohol in early America, Peter Mancall observes that 'many researchers have demonstrated that there is no single response of Indians to alcohol.' Moreover, no genetic trait leads them to drink excessively, and Aboriginal people metabolize alcohol at the same rate as non-Natives. European stereotypes about Native drinking revealed European concerns about excessive drinking in general and the place of Aboriginals in society in particular. The stereotypes were based more on the assumption of the 'unalterable inferiority of Indians' than on observation. In European discourse, alcohol harmed Natives because they were not yet civilized, and the implication was that they probably never would be.[36]

In Canada, as John Tobias notes, legal policy directed at Aboriginal people emphasized protection, civilization, and the eventual elimination of special status through assimilation. Part of the civilizing process was to deny Natives any access to alcohol. Nicholas Simons argues that liquor restrictions imposed on Aboriginal people were not necessarily a result of problems caused by alcohol, although that was often the justification. He sees liquor laws in western Canada as part of the process of subjecting Native people to European rule in order to facilitate European settlement.[37]

Informed by previous colonial and provincial legislation, the federal Indian Act of 1876 incorporated a wide variety of liquor prohibitions. The only authorized way for a Native to use or possess alcohol was to become 'enfranchised' – that is, to become a Canadian citizen and cease to be a status Indian. Even that might not be enough. As Mariana Valverde notes, later liquor provisions of the act in effect broadened the definition of Indian for regulatory purposes. No liquor could be sold or given to anyone 'who follows the Indian mode of life,' even if that person was not legally an Indian.[38]

British Columbia had had legislation pertaining to liquor and Natives on the books since the 1860s, but the primary emphasis of provincial regulation was to uphold federal law. The Government Liquor Act of 1921 denied liquor permits to individuals who fell under the jurisdiction of the Indian Act. Legal paternalism placed Aboriginal people somewhere between minors and interdicts – those denied access to alcohol because of excessive drinking. Unlike minors, however, Natives had no guarantee that they would shed their dependent status. As late as 1959 Chief Charlie Walkem of Spences Bridge lamented, 'My dear people, are we going [to be] under age for all our lives? Are the Indians always going to be under 21?'[39]

In popular discourse, interdiction was often referred to as 'siwashing' – a corruption of 'Salish,' an Aboriginal language group. When the British Columbia Hotels Association (BCHA) banned women from beer parlours in 1926, Reverend R.J. McIntyre of the British Columbia Prohibition Association (BCPA) claimed that the action assaulted the decency of women because it '"Siwashes" them, placing them in the class with Indians and habitual drunkards.'[40]

Temperance supporters had long invoked the firewater myth. At the BCPA's annual convention in 1925, Reverend J. Pearce claimed that unless the illegal liquor traffic was stopped, '26,000 indians [sic] would soon be wiped out.' Later the convention passed a motion that blamed liquor for the problems of Natives and called on Ottawa to 'strictly enforce the law regarding supplying liquor to Indians.' In 1940 R.J. McIntyre warned the LCB against licensing another beer parlour within the vicinity of a reserve in Alert Bay. He added: 'It would appear that Indians have little difficulty in getting liquor these days. There ought to be a closer check on this thing in Vancouver.'[41]

Some Aboriginal people did drink in Vancouver beer parlours. From the early 1930s on, the York Hotel on Howe Street had warned its employees that 'no minors or Indians are to be served, and this must be strictly adhered to.' In 1939 someone unnamed was convicted of supplying beer to a Native in the Dominion Hotel parlour. The LCB cautioned parlour operators to use 'the utmost precaution in serving liquor to Minors and Indians.' By the Second World War the LCB admitted that Natives illegally secured liquor permits, which allowed them to buy liquor. In 1942 the board persuaded Ottawa to stamp 'Indian' on the back of any national registration certificates that were issued to Natives. During the war anyone seeking a liquor permit (to purchase alcohol) required such a certificate. The board advised parlour operators to ask to see the document 'when in doubt' about Natives.[42]

Yet official documents say little about how beer parlours defined and assessed Aboriginals. As James Frideres argues, 'Indian' was a legal category under the Indian Act that changed many times. It did 'not reflect social, cultural, or racial attributes,' and it did not express how First Nations people defined themselves. Parlour workers did not generally rely on identity cards. The only Natives who had any incentive to offer these documents were those enfranchised and thus eligible to drink. 'Indianness' was a constructed assessment based on appearance and behaviour. For example, in 1948 a Mrs K., who was not a status Indian, was denied service in the Regent Hotel because she looked like one. Her friend complained to the LCB, and the secretary replied that 'Mrs. K. is partly of the Indian Race and her facial characteristics are such as to place a waiter in a beer parlour on his guard.' He suggested that Mrs K. obtain an official letter 'to the effect that she is not deemed to be an Indian within the meaning of the Indian Act.'[43]

In November 1949 a constable from the Royal Canadian Mounted Police (RCMP) spotted a status Indian known to him drinking beer in the Pennsylvania Hotel. As a consequence a waiter later pleaded guilty to a charge of illegal service. In the waiter's sworn statement he claimed that he 'had no reason to suspect that he was an Indian.' The waiter thought that the Aboriginal drinker might have been Mexican. His lawyer corroborated that testimony: 'I was looking at the Indian chap and I must confess that I would not have taken him for an Indian myself.' The chief inspector recommended that the licence not be suspended, in part because of the man's alleged non-Native appearance: 'The Indian in question dresses in a very highly respectable manner.'[44]

Behaviour, however, was just as important as appearance in defining Indians. Aboriginal people, even status Indians, who drank quietly and moderately might never be bothered in a beer parlour. They could pass as whites. Assessing the extent of individual passing is impossible. Natives who fooled parlour workers and inspectors were not noted in the records generated by the state. Yet the presence of Aboriginal people in beer parlours was not just the result of passing. In 1950, for example, an LCB undercover agent claimed that he saw, among many infractions, 'an Indian girl' drinking in the Dodson Hotel. He did not associate her with any of the other problems in the parlour. In the warning letter sent to the hotel, the chief inspector never mentioned the woman. She had not caused any trouble and thus, for the moment, was accepted as non-Aboriginal.[45]

With the end of the Second World War the presence of Natives in Vancouver beer parlours acquired more official attention for two related reasons. First, the RCMP intensified its efforts to catch Indians in beer parlours, which often brought it into conflict with provincial liquor authorities. Second, liquor infractions became more prominent as Aboriginal people began to demand equal drinking rights with non-Natives as part of their national campaign for equality without assimilation.

After the war the RCMP appointed a constable to patrol Vancouver's beer parlours. The federal police worked with their city counterparts and with LCB officials. The RCMP's enthusiasm for enforcement, however, often caused friction with the LCB. The board's reaction was not motivated by particular sympathy for Aboriginal drinkers. Provincial regulators believed that the federal police overreacted to the point of setting up or entrapping parlour workers and operators. The tensions between two agencies of the state enhanced the complexities of defining and regulating Indians in beer parlours.[46]

In March 1948, for example, the RCMP arrested a status Indian who was drinking with an enfranchised Native in the Marr Hotel, and a waiter later pleaded guilty to offering illegal service. The chief inspector did not recommend a licence suspension because all had been well until the RCMP showed up. He failed 'to understand why the police just happened to be there when this man was served especially when he was in the company of another Indian not protected by the [Indian] Act.' From the chief inspector's view, had the RCMP not appeared the status Indian would not have existed, since his behaviour had not racialized him.[47]

A similar incident at the Melbourne in April 1949 highlighted the fluidity of definition and enforcement. Two status Indians joined two enfranchised Natives who were drinking beer. The RCMP arrested the status Indians, and a waiter was later convicted of serving liquor illegally. His fellow waiters were angry

because the two status Indians did not order any beer and because one of the two was an employee of the RCMP. Waiters from
other parlours began to contribute fifty cents each to appeal the
case. The chief inspector did not recommend suspension of the
licence because it was 'a borderline case.' He also criticized the
RCMP constable because 'he should have informed the licensee
instead of returning to the Police Station to get other police to
corroborate the drinking.' Technically the officer had acted ap-
propriately, and legally nothing was 'borderline' about the case.
Status Indians who even set foot in beer parlours violated the
liquor act. Yet in this case at least, since they did not drink and
one was an agent of the state, the LCB was willing to accept
them.[48]

Later in 1949, in regard to the November incident at the Pennsylvania Hotel, the chief inspector went further in his criticism of
the RCMP: 'While not wishing to criticize another Government
Department I am of the opinion that the enforcement of this
Indian Act is not being carried out in the correct manner.' He said
that the constable's priority was to 'obtain a conviction instead of
seeing that the Indian was evicted from the premises prior to
receiving any service.' Punishing Aboriginal drinkers appeared
to be the top priority of the RCMP. For provincial authorities,
however, this issue was only one aspect of the complex regulatory process. From the chief inspector's perspective, the RCMP's
narrow focus provoked unfortunate and unnecessary consequences. Therefore he was willing to accept much more latitude
in regulating Aboriginal drinkers, to the point of violating the
liquor act. Defining Natives was thus also related to enforcement
priorities, which differed for federal and provincial authorities.[49]

The RCMP's enthusiasm for enforcement interacted with a
post-war campaign by First Nations for equal access to alcohol.
During the war Aboriginal people served in the armed forces,
where they drank in foreign canteens on the same terms with
non-Natives. As Mary John of the Stoney Creek reserve near
Vanderhoof remembered: 'When those who survived the war
returned to Canada, the Native ex-servicemen found that under
the Indian Act they were still forbidden to drink alcohol any-

where in their own country.' Pressed by Aboriginal groups, the federal government passed a series of amendments to the Indian Act in 1951. As a result, status Indians could drink in a licensed public premise in a province if that province agreed to let Natives drink in such places. In British Columbia the only licensed public premises were beer parlours, and they were opened to all Natives on 15 December 1951. Beer parlours, however, provided the only legal access to alcohol for Natives. They could not buy liquor at government stores. Private clubs – ironically, even licensed veterans' clubs – were still closed to them, and reserves remained officially dry.[50]

Aboriginal leaders immediately criticized the inequality of the changes. Chuck Thorne, a Cowichan chief, captured the sentiments of many: 'It's not right to open the breach a little bit. It should be wide open, same privileges as for whites and same penalties.' Andrew Paull, president of the North American Indian Brotherhood, echoed that thought: 'Indians should have all privileges under B.C. liquor laws and, of course, the same penalties as anyone else.' He added that the new regulations could actually prove to be 'a trap' for Natives, because intoxication on a reserve was still prohibited.[51]

Once beer parlours in Vancouver legally opened their doors to Aboriginal people, status Indians no longer had to pass as whites. Yet the 'beer parlour Indian' did not disappear from the official record. For example, in April 1953 an inspector noted that too much beer (the limit at the time was two glasses per person) had been served to a table 'at which five Indians were seated' in the Melbourne Hotel. The chief inspector wrote a blistering letter to the operator, citing the 'excessive amount of beer on a table where five Indians were seated.' In his letter of apology, the operator admitted that 'an excessive amount of beer was being served on the table where five Indians were seated.' The legal infraction was overservice, not overservice to Indians. Yet too much beer and Native people remained a tenacious conceptual link.[52]

Initially at least, the daily newspapers played on the apparent problems. On Christmas Eve 1951, less than two weeks after parlours opened to Natives, the Vancouver *Province* carried a page-one story under the headline: 'B.C. Indians Roll out Beer Barrel.' The article described a 'howling disorder' in Smithers, BC, after '200 district Indians made first visits to the village's three beer parlors.' With semiotic, if vicious, adroitness, the reporter claimed: 'Squaws carrying papuses [*sic*] on their backs were battling with braves.' The RCMP also argued that opening the beer parlours only increased problems for Natives. The assistant commissioner claimed that 'wherever there are Indians in quantity, close to beer parlours, considerable damage is being done, not only from a general but an economic standpoint.'[53]

Such attitudes were common outside Vancouver, especially in areas with large Native populations. The most spectacular example came from the Tweedsmuir Hotel in Burns Lake, west of Vanderhoof. In February 1952 the Tweedsmuir, which was the only beer parlour in town, applied to open separate toilet facilities for Native women, because, according to the parlour inspector, of 'the reluctence [*sic*] of the white women patrons' to use the same restroom as Native women. The inspector claimed that the reason for the request was that many Native women were 'extremely dirty and infected with various kinds of body lice.' Based on the LCB's response to a similar request from a hotel in Creston, the inspector told the manager of the Tweedsmuir Hotel that 'operators should treat the Indians as they would treat their white patrons patrons under similar circumstances.' Apparently that response did not go over well, because the manager had trouble explaining 'the situation to the local white trade whose regard for the native has never been very high.'[54]

The chief inspector (now called the supervisor of enforcement) denied the request and said that he could 'only repeat my advice which has been given to many licensees throughout this province' – 'Indian women are Canadian citizens [*sic*]; therefore it is not possible for this Board to direct that any discrimination be shown in connection with them when using licensed premises.' Filthy individuals, Aboriginal or white, could be banned from the parlour, but only as individuals. Apparently the chief inspector would not countenance the apartheid that had recently been entrenched in South Africa or the segregation of facilities that was widespread in the United States.[55]

The LCB was obviously under much pressure from non-Aboriginal people opposed to Native people in beer parlours, and the board's refusal to give in appears laudable. Yet such liberalism was more compromised that it might seem. First, the chief inspector informed the hotel manager that he was free to install another toilet for women in the beer parlour. One implication of this suggestion was that facilities could be segregated as long as the LCB was officially unaware of the practice.[56] Second, and more direct, the chief inspector had responded forcefully the previous September (1951) when he learned of dirty workers and filthy conditions in the hotel's dining-room. At that time he had noted, 'It is also alleged that this place is at present being run by Chinese' and supervised by Chinese. He concluded that the 'operators are not deemed to be satisfactory.' In response, the hotel manager closed the dining-room the day after he received the letter, and by the end of October the reopened facilities were being 'operated with all white help.' The LCB certainly had not become colour-blind.[57]

As problems in the Tweedsmuir's beer parlour increased, the local RCMP corporal became noticeably critical of supervision in general and of oversight of Aboriginal drinkers in particular. In response, the hotel's manager de-emphasized the problems allegedly caused by Aboriginal drinkers. He claimed that a more serious problem was that the 'general public' – that is non-Native people – 'particularly in this area do not approve of Indians entering beer parlours.' Consequently they spread misleading information about the comportment of Native people in the local parlour. After a huge influx of Aboriginal people – some 350 to 400, according to the hotel – for the 1 July holiday in 1952, the manager claimed that 'without exaggeration there was hardly an argument.' The RCMP corporal, in contrast, recommended that the parlour be shut down.[58]

Initially, at least, the local parlour inspector sided with the hotel. Based on his observations and interviews, he concluded that he could not support the corporal's reports. He also specu-

lated that some of the white residents' complaints were motivated more by short beer service than by problems caused by
Aboriginal people.[59]

Everything changed in November 1952 after the arrival in
Burns Lake of a new RCMP corporal, whom the inspector found
more congenial, and, more important, after a Saturday-night fracas that involved Native patrons. The inspector said that the
parlour operators had done the best they could and that the
trouble had started after they had refused service to intoxicated
Native people who had illegally consumed hard liquor before
they entered the facility. After the incident the local magistrate,
the RCMP, the hotel managers, the band chief, and thirty other
Native people met to discuss the incident. On the recommendation of the magistrate, the inspector said, 'It was the concurred
opinion that natives should be barred' from the parlour for at
least two months. He added that the chief had seconded the
motion and that a majority of the 'older natives present' supported the ban. Once in place, however, the ban became indefinite, and in May 1953 the inspector reported that the operators
did not intend 'to permit the native [sic] to return, providing the
Board does not object.' The chief inspector, who earlier would
not support segregated toilets, merely passed on the reports to
the LCB's chairman without comment.[60]

The ban against Native drinkers was still in effect in May 1954
when L.G. Saul, the magistrate who had made the initial recommendation, told a conference of BC magistrates that Native people would be kept out of the Tweedsmuir Hotel's beer parlour
'for their own good.' The comment outraged Andrew Paull, who
argued that they could be banned only through individual interdiction. Magistrate Saul asked rhetorically, 'What's the difference
of interdicting them one at a time or all at once?'[61]

Since early 1952 Paull also had been engaged in a simmering
feud with the RCMP over alleged discriminatory enforcement
against Native people in the Prince Rupert division. In November 1953 an inspector obliquely commented on the dispute in
reference to the situation at the Grandview Hotel in South
Hazelton, near Terrace: 'There are a large number of natives in

this area but their presence in the Licensed Premises is not particularly encouraged as they have been hard to manage in the past. However[,] increased action by the RCMP ... against drunkeness [sic] etc has resulted in over 275 prosecutions this year and said action has had a very salutory [sic] effect.'[62]

Assessing the intoxication of Aboriginal people for purposes of law enforcement was a subjective process. A non-Native MLA for Prince Rupert said that police and magistrates in his community determined Natives' intoxication simply by the presence of any breath odour of liquor. He added that the new regulations actually reinforced stereotypes about Natives and liquor because legal drinking could take place only in parlours, and any consequent problems were quite visible. Mary John remembered that 'people would drink as much as they could before closing time, because they knew that once they left the beer parlor, the only place they could drink was in some back alley or beside the railway tracks.'[63]

Two scholarly studies in the 1950s both argued that the partial lifting of liquor restrictions had done nothing to decrease the bitterness that Native people felt because of the lack of equal treatment. Edwin Lemert of the University of California interviewed Natives on the BC mainland coast and on Vancouver Island. He concluded that they felt 'a deep sense of injustice because they are fined and sent to provincial prison for drinking, a pleasure which white persons enjoy with impunity.' For many Natives, 'drinking has become associated with political consciousness and has grown into a symbol of native solidarity.' A study sponsored by the federal government and led by anthropologist Harry Hawthorn of the University of British Columbia reached a similar assessment: 'There can be no doubt that many Indians strongly resent the denial to them of full liquor privileges.' This study recommended 'that the Indian of British Columbia should be in no different a position from the White citizen of British Columbia in respect to liquor laws.'[64]

While both books assumed that liquor equality would facilitate assimilation, neither blithely accepted the firewater myth.

Both stressed that Aboriginal people, like non-Natives, had diverse drinking patterns and attitudes towards alcohol. Some Natives oriented to temperance saw the opening of beer parlours as a 'white' trick to demoralize and bankrupt them. Many others drank to excess for a variety of reasons, while some incorporated alcohol into traditional activities. At first Mary John enjoyed meeting her husband and friends in the Vanderhoof beer parlour. The novelty wore off in 1957 after a young couple was killed in a train accident in which alcohol was a major factor. She never had another drink. Andrew Paull was one of the most vocal advocates for the end of discrimination in drinking, but he had no personal interest in beer: 'I am not a beer drinker – hate the stuff.' Yet he strongly believed that Natives themselves should decide what to, where to, and whether to drink. BC First Nations achieved equal access to alcohol in 1962, nearly 15 years after they had received the provincial franchise and two years after the federal franchise. The final liquor provisions of the Indian Act, however, were not removed until 1985.[65]

Conclusion

Creating and regulating the unwanted in Vancouver beer parlours constituted a multilevel process based on laws, practices, appearance, and behaviour. In some cases, 'passing' best described that behaviour, and in beer parlours passing was most closely associated with minors and status Indians. They were the only groups explicitly barred on the basis of legal definition. Yet appropriate behaviour allowed them to act as whites or adults.

Behaviour, however, was often more negotiated, or at least interactive, than simple passing conveys. Provincial and federal authorities did not consistently enforce the proscription against status Indians, as they did not always share the same priorities. Some state officials might still accept an Aboriginal person who did not necessarily pass, or did not even try to. Consequently 'Indian,' like 'minor,' was defined more by context than by legal text, and both were flexible categories.

To a certain extent parlour decency was linked to the behavioural reputation of Asians, especially the Chinese. Because of their alleged ties to vice, Chinese were not eligible to operate or work in beer parlours, even after they won the franchise. Their absence, or invisibility, signified at least some respectability for parlours. Yet with the toleration if not the blessing of the state, Chinese permeated the margins of parlours as janitors and of hotels as room operators and owners. In a regulatory sense, these people were less racialized because their behaviour did not directly compromise the parlours.

The racialized gender relations in beer parlours often brought behaviour and appearance together. While some facilities discriminated simply on the basis of appearance, such discrimination officially was less acceptable after the Second World War. Thus men of colour could drink in some parlours without too much difficulty – unless white women accompanied them. That behaviour racialized both the men of colour and the white women. Much official and popular antipathy was directed at them, but 'mixed-race' couple was a narrow construction based on the fear of miscegenation and the sullying of whiteness. The antipathy towards such pairings underscored the privileged status of heterosexual, Anglo-Celtic men. Despite reality, a mixed-race couple that did not include a white woman did not exist as an official category of concern.

Finally, citizenship helped to define and regulate the unwanted. In practice it was tied to national origins or ethnicity, and people from southern and eastern Europe were not quite Canadian, even if they could vote. Yet they were Canadian enough to work in or own parlours. Citizenship requirements were more harshly directed at both Asians and Aboriginal people. These restrictions were not only racial but also elastic. The formal conferring of the franchise certainly did not guarantee equality, or even access to the parlours, whether individuals were patrons, workers, or operators. Citizenship was a political process tied to concepts of parlour decency. It is to the politics of regulation that we turn in the next chapter.

Chapter Five

Reconfiguring Decency in the 1950s: The Politics of Regulation

Interviewed in his room at the Hotel Vancouver in July 1949, British journalist Noel Monks commented on his unsuccessful attempt to order a beer while standing at the service counter in a beer parlour. He said that Canada was 'a tremendous, virile country and I know from personal experience that your fighting men can match the finest in the world. Yet you've apparently let yourselves be legislated into a state of adolescence when it comes to the use of alcohol.' Monks described such regulation as 'just one step from making you stand out in the rain and hold up your arm and shout, "Heil Ottawa."' Battle-tested virility had given way to impotent adolescence because of the fascism of beer parlour regulation. Something had changed in the post-war discourse of liquor regulation.[1]

After the Second World War regulation of beer parlours became part of a larger political debate on public drinking in British Columbia that culminated in a new liquor act in 1954. From one perspective, politics can be seen as a state-centred process – in this case, first a plebiscite in June 1952, then a commission of inquiry in the last half of 1952, and finally new legislation (passed in early 1953 and proclaimed a year later) in response to a variety of interest groups. The obvious conclusions are that wet opinions prevailed, and the state certified them with additional licensed public facilities to compete with beer parlours. This perspective on politics is worthy of discussion because regulation of public drinking did change. At the same time, however, it offers only a narrow view of how regulation worked. The dynamics of regulation are better understood with a broader vision of politics.

Politics also consists of contests over knowledge about public drinking that went beyond the state. Parlour regulation had always been as much about naming space and the people who occupied it as about controlling drinking. Regulation was a way to order reality through the power of naming. Yet regulators also created knowledge so that they could use that knowledge. Decency not only defined people but also was the rationalization with which to act on or discriminate against people. As we saw above, regulation involved many actors, including those regulated, who promoted their own versions of decency.

After the war one can see a reconfiguration of the discourse of decency – in effect, a new knowledge of public drinking. Particularly promoted by the press, restaurants, and cabarets, this knowledge emphasized the respectability of public drinking, as long as it occurred in a decent environment that encouraged moderation. That environment, however, was no longer the beer parlour, if it ever had been. This new knowledge condemned parlours as indecent working-class centres of excess. Moreover, the state stood out for particular reproach. An antiquated liquor act and inefficient, indeed corrupt, administration retarded decency by confining legal public drinking to beer parlours.

Promoters of this new knowledge offered the cocktail lounge as a post-war, modern counterpoint to the beer parlour. When lounges opened in Vancouver in 1954, they operated with fewer formal constraints and less surveillance than parlours. They catered to a middle-class clientele and neither expected nor welcomed beer parlour patrons. Cocktail customers could be expected to discipline themselves to a far greater extent than parlour patrons. For example, in lounges women and men could drink together. Yet even there formal and informal methods still regulated gender relations, and women continued to be more regulated than men.

Beer parlours remained, but they were now more morally marginalized. Moral marginalization was closely linked to class, but the class implications can be read in more than one way. On the one hand, one can emphasize the failure of beer parlours rather than condemn the people who frequented them. After all, many wage workers themselves were decidedly unhappy with the parlours, and some considered them sites of excessive consumption. Moreover, as hostile as the inquiry commissioners of 1952 were towards beer parlours, they were sympathetic to some sort of 'workingman's club' for the moderate consumption of draft beer. The daily newspapers, some of the strongest champions of cocktails, even appealed to the myth of the British pub, which they saw as a homey environment where respectable working people gathered for sociability and a pint.

On the other hand, from the day they opened their doors, critics condemned parlours as suspect space patronized by suspect people. The defenders of parlours argued that the right environment would promote decency among the working-class patrons. Implicit in that defence was the assumption that without regulation working people would not conform to decency's expectations of moderate consumption, appropriate comportment, and heterosexual propriety. Parlour patrons championed their own definitions of decency, but eventually at a cost. After the war critics argued that parlours had failed because they had not been able to remould working-class drinkers.

'Reconfiguring Knowledge'

Compared with the First World War, the 1939–45 conflict was decidedly wet. The drys were at best only partially able to link their cause to the war effort. The first war had acted as a catalyst for a movement growing in popularity. By the beginning of the Second World War, prohibition had not only been dead for nearly twenty years in British Columbia, it had also been spectacularly discredited in the United States, which abandoned it in 1933. Moreover, liquor interests on both sides of the border embarked on public relations campaigns that included raising fears about the return of prohibition. The most important BC wartime restrictions on liquor were the result of shortages and rationing, not the continued efforts of temperance groups. Even many non-drinkers bought their meagre allotment of alcohol to sell or give away during rationing. Moreover, young men and women learned to drink in military canteens. After the war, with the return home of military personnel, continued prosperity, and the end of rationing, liquor consumption soared. The dry years were a generation away in the past.[2]

Mariana Valverde argues that by the time of the Second World War, especially in the United States, 'there was a major shift in the ethics of drinking.' The foundation of that sea change was the growing acceptance, at least among the elite, of the ideas that pleasure was normal and that morality was not based on the suppression of desire. Rather than favouring temperance, experts in alcohol studies now cautiously promoted moderate drinking, or what Valverde describes as enlightened hedonism. Like other forms of consumption, drinking was a potentially positive way to promote relaxation and social interaction.[3]

In Vancouver, however, beer parlours were the material legacy of the prohibition era. They were the only licensed facilities where the general public could legally drink. Vancouver's parlours had remained largely unchanged since they first opened. They still offered no food, no entertainment, and no beverage except beer, not even soft drinks. Parlours had if anything become even more restrictive during the war, with supper-hour closings and the installation of partitions to isolate unattached men from unattached women. As well, Vancouver's parlours tended to be quite crowded, as no new ones had been licensed.

Post-war critics condemned the facility as a promoter of the excessive consumption that it was designed to curtail. The first critic to gain prominence in the press was the Right Reverend Harold E. Sexton, Anglican bishop of British Columbia, who was a strong supporter of liberalized drink reform. In the summer of 1945 he criticized the liquor act for herding people 'into beer parlors where they may do nothing but guzzle.' The Vancouver *Province* echoed these sentiments by describing beer parlours as 'those dismal and melancholy resorts' and later as 'sterilized filling stations.' Provincial politicians fuelled the criticism. Herbert

Gargrave, the Co-operative Commonwealth Federation (CCF) member of the legislature from the northern constituency of Mackenzie, claimed that what people wanted from beer parlours was 'an evening's entertainment, an evening's sociability.' Instead, 'What do they get? Just plain drunk very often.' His colleague Nancy Hodges (Victoria member of the Coalition – a 1941–51 alliance of Liberals and Conservatives) said that beer parlours should be closed because 'first, last and foremost they are aimed at the encouragement of drinking for drinking's sake.'[4]

Rather than closing the parlours, the more common suggestion was to open additional licensed public facilities, especially cocktail lounges. Here spirits and wine could be served by the glass in an elegant environment enhanced by food and entertainment. In 1947, the year in which Ontario began to allow cocktail lounges, the chairman of the BC Liquor Control Board (LCB) sent a list of suggested changes to the attorney general, including licensed hotel lounges and restaurants. A national Gallup poll in 1949 claimed that support for cocktails was the strongest in British Columbia. According to its results, lounges were most popular with 'White collar' and 'Business and profess.' people. Their supporters invoked cocktail lounges as a new model of decent public drinking, dismissing the idea that beer was necessarily a drink of moderation. Cocktail lounges would be the domain of the respectable middle class, whose restrained consumption of spirits would contrast with the excessive beer swilling of the parlours' clientele.[5]

The most organized promoters of cocktails were the restaurants and cabarets. For decades restaurant owners had argued that eating places provided an ideal place for liquor service because of the moderating effect of food. As one restaurant official put it: 'Temperance in the consumption of alcoholic beverages can best be helped by serving of liquor by the glass along with food.' Owners also raised the more self-interested consideration that if hotel restaurants obtained cocktail licences, then fairness dictated that all restaurants should be eligible for them.[6]

Even more prominent with their demands were the unlicensed cabarets, which had operated for years in Vancouver. The Commodore Ballroom had opened on Granville Street in 1929, and the Cave, on Hornby Street, in 1937. After the war, cabarets became even more popular, and people regularly drank in them, despite the law. Patrons brought their own bottles of liquor, stored them under the table, and bought expensive 'set-ups' of glasses, ice, and mixers. The newspapers often referred to these cabarets as 'bottle clubs.' The central downtown venues, such as the Cave, the Palomar Supper Club on Burrard, and the Pano-rama Roof in the Hotel Vancouver, all appealed to a middle-class crowd. Yet periodically the police raided the clubs, seized bottles, and occasionally arrested revellers. By the late 1940s cabaret owners were claiming that they welcomed such raids as strength-ening their efforts to show that the liquor laws were unenforce-able and 'antiquated.' Their proposed solution was to license cabarets to sell cocktails by the glass. Licensed cabarets, they argued, would promote moderation, as people would have a few drinks by the glass rather than draining the bottles hidden under the table.[7]

Criticism of the legal fiction of private clubs also motivated the push for cocktail lounges. Since the 1920s private clubs had been licensed to allow members to keep and consume their personal liquor. Technically not open to the general public, clubs could offer food, some entertainment, games, and even accommoda-tion. In 1947 the government licensed clubs to sell liquor to members and their guests. The result was a rapid expansion of cheap memberships in downtown Vancouver. For example, the Pacific Athletic Club on Howe Street had some 3,000 'members' by 1948. The Vancouver *Sun* decried the hypocrisy of clubs and said: 'The sensible thing to do would be to legalize the sale of liquor by the glass in cocktail bars or night clubs, as they do in civilized communities.' Civilization was only a short drive away. Neighbouring Washington state had allowed the sale of beer and wine in restaurants since 1934, and in 1948 voters there approved an initiative in favour of the cocktail 'room.'[8]

Early in 1952 the BC attorney general announced a plebiscite on liquor for the next general election. The language of the plebi-scite framed the debate: 'Are you in favour of the sale of spirituous liquor and wine by the glass in establishments licensed for such purpose?' Voters were in effect asked if they wanted a legal alternative to licensed public drinking in beer parlours.[9]

Temperance groups organized opposition. The way the 'no' side constructed its case showed how much the discourse on public drinking had shifted. In the 1920s and 1930s the drys had championed another plebiscite on public drinking. After the war they argued for a commission of inquiry, which, they argued, would help prevent uninformed voters from making the wrong choice. In 1950 the British Columbia Temperance League (BCTL) suggested that 'the present state of public information is not such that a socially useful answer would be likely to result from a plebiscite.' Just before the government released the text of the plebiscite, the BCTL urged the attorney general at least to establish a 'research committee to present factual material to the citizens of the province [that would enable] them to vote with full knowledge of the case.'[10]

Temperance leaders also were careful to reorder their knowledge of public drinking. The word 'temperance' no longer elicited much moral fervour, so the drys opted for the post-war language of science. In cooperation with the Vancouver Council of Churches, the BCTL created the Alcohol Research Council to spearhead the 'no' campaign. The choice of a scientific-sounding name was quite intentional. The chair of the BCTL's policy committee emphasized objectivity and 'finding out the facts and allowing them to speak for themselves.' The president of the BCTL, who became executive director of the new council, resigned his temperance position so that the 'yes' side could not argue that the council was 'merely a camouflage organization working for the militant "drys."'[11]

The wets were just as careful in organizing their campaign to construct a new view of public drinking. Under the direction of the former advertising director of the Vancouver *Sun*, supporters of cocktails created the Citizens' Committee for a Common Sense Liquor Law. Once again Washington state probably had some influence. Supporters of the successful 1948 cocktail initiative had called their proposal 'The Common Sense Bill.' In British

Columbia the wets stressed that the current liquor law was 'outdated' and proposed to 'modernize it in the public interest.' They presented a 'yes' vote as being a vote not just for change but also for a 'saner system for the sale of liquor.' The rhetoric was powerful. Those 'citizens' who were 'modern' and governed by 'common sense' supported cocktails. They would restore sanity and respect for the law by replacing an antiquated system of licensed public drinking dominated by beer parlours. The *Sun* itself blamed the regulatory status quo for 'lawlessness and depravity.'[12]

On 12 June 1952, British Columbians cast 316,266 ballots in favour of the plebiscite and 204,761 against. In Vancouver nearly 65 per cent of the votes were for the 'yes' side. The general secretary of the Canadian Temperance Federation, who had been in the province to help the 'no' side, managed to find something encouraging in the results. He said that the voters were 'not satisfied with the present set-up, – i.e. Beer Parlours. They want a change for the better.' Ironically, the provincial election resulted in a temperance-leaning government led by Social Crediter W.A.C. Bennett, whose first action on public drinking was to appoint a full commission of inquiry.[13]

The Liquor Inquiry Commission

The three-member commission consisted of H.H. Stevens, former Conservative MP and president of the Vancouver Board of Trade; George Home, secretary of the British Columbia Federation of Labour; and Very Reverend Cecil Swanson, dean of Vancouver's Christ Church Cathedral. Before the commission the status quo received little support. The majority of briefs supported the licensing of additional public facilities. Temperance groups sought to limit new outlets, but they also wanted more restrictions on parlours.[14]

The strongest defender of beer parlours was Local 676, the Beverage Dispensers Union. The union had long claimed that the regulatory system worked well, and it had actively campaigned against the plebiscite. Its leaders argued that additional facilities would threaten the wages and working conditions of their members. The most change the union was willing to accept was a limited number of hotel cocktail bars and liquor service in cabarets.[15]

In the midst of the liquor hearings in 1952, Local 676 decided to become actively involved in the March of Dimes charity campaign. The union wanted 'to bring forth to the public that we can raise money for charitable purposes, bringing goodwill and good fellowship before the public eye.' Parlour workers inaugurated what became the Bartenders Blitz – an annual fund-raising event. Their choice of dress was significant. They wore a stylized 'old time bartenders costume' while they collected donations in beer parlours. Their traditional saloon titles and garb now invoked nostalgia rather than condemnation, generating a more positive resonance than the white coat and black tie that they normally wore. Moreover, the charity, sometimes referred to informally as the Mothers' March of Dimes, was appreciative and seemed content to be associated with workers whose main activity was selling liquor. Maternal reformers of the early twentieth century probably rolled over in their graves.[16]

Continuation of the existing beer parlours mustered only luke-warm support from other sectors of organized labour. Soon after the war the Vancouver and District Labour Council had given a slight nod in favour of hotel cocktail lounges, but it particularly wanted more and better beer parlours. One official described existing facilities as 'large, noisy, unhomey and unenjoyable em-poriums,' packed with men and women who consumed 'infi-nitely more beer ... than is either good for them or enjoyable.' Appearing before the commission, the Canadian Brotherhood of Railway Employees went a step further and said that if women were allowed to serve liquor standards of conduct would im-prove. The British Columbia Hotels Association (BCHA) later threatened to sue the Retail Clerks Union after one of its execu-tive members allegedly said that parlours were 'still run like hog troughs ... Parlors aren't fit for decent people to enter.' These were hardly ringing endorsements of what were suppose to be working-class social centres.[17]

The BCHA also appeared before the commission to defend its

parlours. Wary of how the press would present its views, the association published its complete submission as an advertisement in the *Province*. To widespread criticism of the parlours, it responded that overall they were well-run, tightly regulated, and continuously inspected. Their problems were largely beyond the control of their operators. The association recommended that parlours be allowed to sell snack foods and soft drinks, as well as providing wired music or television as distractions from drinking. Most significant, however, it claimed that the facilities were still important to their patrons. The brief described the beer parlour as 'the poor man's club' and 'the only social club for most people of average means.' It was a place where 'anyone may spend a sociable hour or two at a very small cost and one that does not interfere with the support of home and family.'[18]

While the commissioners claimed to have open minds on the subject of liquor, their critique of parlours was consistently prominent. They 'bombarded' the BCHA's representatives with 'questions ... about the conduct of sub-standard hotels.' Some parlours, Chairman Stevens claimed, were 'not hotels in any sense of the word. They're a disgrace to the community.' Late in November 1952 he toured four Vancouver waterfront parlours. He said that he 'saw hundreds of absolute drunks. I saw men staggering in slumping down in chairs and getting glasses piled up in front of them.'[19]

In their report, the commissioners did not place the entire blame on the hotels. They also criticized the province's brewers and the LCB. The called Vancouver-area brewers before the commission to explain bank-loan guarantees on behalf of parlours. The commissioners doubted the brewers' assertion that the loans were for renovations. Vancouver Breweries, for example, had loaned $30,000 to the Haddon Hotel on Powell Street, a place that the chairman described as 'a row of rooms in a shack, rooms eight by ten – in fact I was in one about six by eight.' The real purpose of the loans, he argued, was to make sure that a parlour used only its benefactor's draft beer. Breweries that guaranteed a parlour's debt could exert power over it beyond the formal regulations.[20]

While loan guarantees were another form of parlour regulation that went beyond the state, the state facilitated that regulation. Many jurisdictions outlawed so-called tied houses – that is, they made it illegal for brewers and distillers to have a financial interest in licensed premises. British Columbia's Government Liquor Act, however, did not explicitly ban tied houses. Moreover, while in theory a parlour could sell whatever draft beer it chose, LCB policy dictated that it could offer only one brand at a time, and an operator had to file an application with the board to change brands. This restriction encouraged a parlour operator to become tied to a particular brewery.[21]

The commission's report also held the LCB partly responsible for conditions in beer parlours. It pointed out that the LCB was in reality a 'one-man Board,' which resulted in 'obvious faulty administration.' It accused the board and the inspectors of ignoring the regulations against serving drunks and minors. In addition, inspectors were 'not unaware of the deplorable conditions that mark the day-to-day operations of the beer parlours.' The report said that the 'charitable' explanation was that the inspectors were 'grossly incompetent.' The 'alternative' explanation was that the inspectors' actions stemmed from 'sinister disregard of duty.' This statement was as far as the commissioners were willing to go in assessing the extent of corruption in the LCB. They concluded that it was not their duty to 'delve into the reasons' for the board's administrative problems.[22]

Certainly 'liquor regulation' and 'corruption' had been linked rhetorically since government control began in 1921. Yet what constituted corruption was definitely open to interpretation and had long stirred public discussion and newspaper coverage. Most commonly observers associated it with political patronage, which to those who received it seemed the just reward for faithful party work.

The presence of the state tended to make liquor regulation seem black and white, like the codified law on which it was based. Beneath the surface, however, patronage and corruption once again underscored the multifaceted qualities of regulation.

Regulation went beyond formal legality. In some ways corruption undercut the power of state regulation and thus was
anantithetical to it. Yet corruption was an interactive process that
engaged state and non-state actors. The main outcome of this
symbiotic relationship was an enhanced status quo. As well,
corruption, rather than promoting chaos or disorder, created different kinds of regulations, some more visible than others.[23]

The daily newspapers offered themselves as a moral opposition to this less-visible regulation. After the government licensed
private clubs to sell liquor to members and guests in 1947, press
attacks on corruption became more pointed. In June 1948, for
example, *Sun* reporter Jack Webster found that he could buy
drinks in most Vancouver clubs, even though he was not a member of any of them. His lurid account appeared under the headline, 'Club Bars "Open to All."' Beside it, a front-page editorial
invoked the discredited language of prohibition to condemn 'The
Speakeasy Mentality' of public drinking.

More seriously, the newspapers alleged that the real locus of
regulation was not the LCB's offices in Victoria but the provincial
electoral riding of Vancouver Centre – a Liberal stronghold long
described as the corrupt power base of the party. A disgruntled,
anonymous parlour operator supported their critique. In the late
1940s the operator had sent the leader of the opposition – Harold
Winch of the CCF – a scathing seventy-page critique of liquor
regulation. He charged that a Vancouver cabal, based in the
Quadra Club on Seymour Street, controlled all aspects of formal
parlour regulation, including licensing, beer purchases, suspen-
sions, and required improvements. His accusations, however,
were never made public.[24]

Newspapers, however, had a more symbiotic relationship with
alleged corruption than it would appear. The daily press operated in a competitive market increasingly depending more on
advertising revenue than on links with any particular political
party. Sensational accounts of liquor corruption attracted readers
and thus advertising dollars. Moreover, the press used corruption to order their knowledge of public drinking. The Vancouver
papers in particular were strong advocates of liberalized public

drinking. In the above example from the *Sun* on club drinking, the paper concluded that the lesson learned was that 'the law should be changed.' According to the paper, licensed cocktail lounges or nightclubs would 'comply with the moral standards of the people as a whole.' With a moral nudge, the paper suggested: 'An honest government wouldn't debate the matter for a second.'[25]

While the liquor commission's report did not comment specifically on corruption and patronage, its general recommendations emphasized honesty and accountability in liquor regulation. It called specifically for the end of tied houses and recommended that all beer parlours and many 'private' clubs have their licences cancelled. As a fresh start, all would have to reapply and adhere to the requirements of the new act once it was passed.[26]

The commissioners still saw a future for the beer parlour, but in an altered form. They had no patience with many existing Vancouver hotel parlours, which they believed promoted 'debauchery' rather than offering a 'comfortable and decent' place for refreshment. Yet they accepted the argument that beer was 'the least offensive of all alcoholic beverages' and that an 'overwhelming demand' existed for the '"workingman's club" type of beverage-room.' They recommended that beer by the glass, snack foods, and soft drinks be sold in public houses 'whether associated with a hotel or not.'[27]

The commissioners were also wary of the 'exotic, dimly lighted, voluptuous type of cocktail bar which creates a delusive impression of social distinction.' Mainly to satisfy the demands of the tourist industry, they were willing to accept some 'beverage lounges,' primarily in upscale hotels. They also recommended a limited number of licensed restaurants and cabarets.[28]

The Government Liquor Act of 1953

Symbolically at least, the government responded quickly to the criticism of beer parlours raised in the commission's report. In January 1953 the attorney general ordered that only one beer at a time be served to a customer. Parlour workers were unhappy with the order, because it increased their workload and customers objected to it. After meeting with a delegation from the Beverage Dispensers Union, the attorney general agreed to restore the two-glass limit, provided that the customer actually requested the second glass. At the same time he announced that parlours would be required to sell snack foods and soft drinks. He said that these changes would promote moderation.[29]

Because of an intervening election, a year passed before a new Government Liquor Act was proclaimed in January 1954. Beer parlours were to be replaced by so-called public houses, which would still sell only beer, but would no longer necessarily be attached to hotels. The act's regulations placed additional emphasis on making parlours brighter and less crowded. Moderation was to be promoted with diversions, including packaged food, radio, and television. Licensees were specifically prohibited from treating, although customers could still treat among themselves.[30]

The overall environment changed little. Patrons still had to sit at tables and leave for at least an hour at supper-time. The segregated sections remained, and women continued to be banned from serving beer. Parlour workers had expressed much anxiety among themselves about the possibility of women servers, and Local 676 lobbied the government to maintain the ban. The obvious labour concerns were that female servers might be difficult to organize, would drive down wages, and cost men their jobs. Yet women servers were also an affront to the work culture of the parlour employees.and their union. According to the union, theirs was 'the oldest in the city and the strongest,' and the members feared that women would drain the union's vitality. Some members continued to criticize even the presence of women in parlours. Jack Johnson, at seventy-five years old still a waiter in the Princeton Hotel's parlour, remembered his days in the old saloons. He claimed, 'There wasn't half the trouble there is today.' Saloons were better than parlours 'because there were no women allowed in the bars in those days.'[31]

Vancouver's parlours also remained in their existing hotel locations. The new act allowed old licences to continue in force until the end of 1954. In June the attorney general informed the chairman of the Manitoba Liquor Inquiry Commission that the government would confine parlours 'as far as circumstances will permit to operating hotels.' The government had been persuaded by the parlour operators' argument that they had made huge investments in hotel facilities that should not be jeopardized unnecessarily. The government also had no interest in licensing what the attorney general referred to as 'taverns' – free-standing drinking establishments that offered nothing else to their communities.[32]

Even before the year ended, the government was being severely criticized for its administration of the new liquor act. Two of the former inquiry commissioners said that it had ignored many of their recommendations. As well, the chairman of the 'yes' committee argued that restaurants outside hotels had been discriminated against because they could serve only beer and wine with meals, rather than the more popular and profitable cocktails. Neither cabaret operators nor their workers were happy with the severe licensing restrictions placed on their facilities, which discouraged owners from even applying for licences. In January 1954 the *News-Herald* had titled one editorial 'At Last, a Civilized Liquor System in BC.' By March it resorted to Cold War language with an editorial headlined, 'Now – A Cocktail Curtain?' in reaction to the paper's inability to find out who had applied for cocktail licences. The headline of a *Province* editorial in June lamented, 'This Isn't What the People Voted For.'[33]

Cocktail Lounges: Mixed Messages

Despite their criticism of the operation of the new liquor act, the newspapers recognized cocktail lounges as a significant shift in licensed public drinking. Hotel lounges, which first opened in Vancouver in July 1954, were designed to make 'possible respectable drinking in respectable places,' according to the *Sun*. In cocktail lounges decency was not explicitly linked to entertainment, food, or membership, as in cabarets, restaurants, or clubs.

Like parlours, lounges were places to drink. As well, lounge decency was defined by the naming of public space and the people who occupied it. Yet the design of a lounge and the expectation of who would drink there intentionally set it apart from the beer parlour.[34]

For example, the regulations actually required that a cocktail lounge have a bar where customers could drink. The *News-Herald* found this feature noteworthy enough for a front-page story headlined 'Bars Back in BC after 3 Decades.' Public drinking at bars had not legally existed since the parlours had opened in 1925. What that lounge bar represented, however, was not entirely clear. Part of the problem, as Mariana Valverde notes, was that no one had been explicit as to the core problem of the old saloon bars. Was it their design, or the opportunities that they offered for sociability and fast service, or the fact that drinkers stood up? This ambiguity in the new cocktail lounges was evident in the requirement that the service bar have seats where patrons would sit. The bar had returned, but not the old saloon bar.[35]

Yet the ambiguity went further, or, more probably, enlightened hedonism went only so far in 1954. As Doug Owram cautions, in Canada 'the 1950s were [still] a conservative age.' In lounges, customers mainly sat at small tables. Separate booths were banned, and every person had to be able to see everyone else. Visibility would be enhanced by the requirement that lounges, like all licensed premises, be as brightly lit as the average kitchen. Regulation had assumed different forms, but the opening of cocktail lounges certainly did not mean the end of regulation.[36]

Lounges were also decent places to drink because they discouraged working people from patronizing them. The could not sell draft beer, the workers' cheap drink. It remained confined to beer parlours and was the only alcoholic beverage exempt from sales tax. In lounges, bartenders poured mixed drinks that cost at least five times as much as a ten-cent glass of draft beer. Lounges also had expectations about comportment that discouraged workers. Dress codes were common, and even drinking itself required special knowledge, as cocktails could be quite complex drinks.

As Joseph Lanza notes, cocktails were linked to class-based images of the good life, and, in the United States at least, by 'the fifties cocktails became a talisman for urban sophisticates on the move.'[37]

These class implications were not lost on observers. Early in the debate over lounges, Independent Labour MLA Tom Uphill had said that cocktail lounges 'would be discrimination against the workingman.' As much as it supported lounges, the *Province* wanted more than 'flossy cocktail bars.' It offered its explanation in explicit class terms: 'There are thousands of British Columbians who want to be able to have a drink in their working clothes and they would hardly feel at home in such surroundings ... We want some "pubs" in the British tradition.' As well, labour leaders in Vancouver claimed that lounges did little for 'the workingman' because they were 'too high-priced for him.'[38]

A cocktail lounge closely linked class and gender. Its clients did not have their sexuality regulated as closely as did parlour patrons. For example, while women could not serve liquor in lounges, the two sexes could drink together. No segregated drinking areas were required – partitions were prohibited. These changes reflected less proscriptive attitudes in general after the war, especially towards alcohol, leisure, and gender interaction. Yet lounge regulation was also a consequence of conceptions of lounges as respectable, middle-class facilities. In working-class beer parlours separate sections for men and for ladies and escorts were required for nearly another decade.[39]

Still, lounges did regulate sexuality spatially. They could not have stalls or boxes, known more colloquially as 'necking booths.' As well, as in parlours, women were more regulated than men were, and not just by the state. When Victoria's first lounge opened in 1954, a reporter observed that only solitary men occupied the bar stools. Women sat only at the tables. By the late 1950s the lounge in the Sylvia Hotel, Vancouver's first, banned solitary women as a house rule.[40]

Cocktail lounges also reinforced the ambiguous dilemmas of middle-class, heterosexual masculinity in the 1950s. The dominant social view in both Canada and the United States was that men had to conform to the dictates of profession, marriage, and parenthood. Yet individuality was also important, because too much conformity could lead to passivity, even feminization. Walking the fine line of independent conformity created much anxiety, which could inspire a man to head to the lounge, especially after work before he went home. Yet, unlike the stereotype of his working-class counterpart, a middle-class man could not drink heavily to reinforce masculinity. Excessive consumption was hardly the sign of an urban sophisticate. Moreover, some psychiatrists argued that alcohol abuse was a marker of repressed homosexuality, and most experts agreed that problem drinking was at least a sign of deficient masculinity.[41]

The cocktail lounge was hardly a site of uncomplicated masculinity. Lounges were not only designed to include women, they also regendered spirits or hard liquor. A dry martini was essentially straight gin, but many cocktails were coloured, decorated, or flavoured to appeal to women. Yet some, such as daiquiris, Mai Tais, and Singapore Slings, became popular with both sexes. Ernest Hemingway, self-styled man among men, had a fondness for frozen daiquiris – but doubles, of course. *Playboy* magazine, which promoted cocktails as part of the essential decor of the urban male apartment, questioned drinks with umbrellas and the environment in which they were consumed. One *Playboy* writer said that cocktails with the 'hues and flavors of cake frosting' imbibed at delicate Chinese tables were a sign of 'general male emasculation.'[42]

The *Province*'s reference to 'flossy' cocktail bars had more than class implications. Even before the first lounge opened in Vancouver, the newspaper offered two editorials in two weeks that stressed that British Columbia was a province of working men. 'Working men' did not mean middle-class professionals of suspect masculinity who wanted to drink in cocktail lounges. Working men were 'fishermen, loggers, miners, construction men' who drank in beer parlours. Obviously beer parlours had to change for many reasons, and one of them, as Noel Monks had emphasized, was that overregulation had sapped the virility of the men who drank in them. Cocktail lounges were 'fine for people who like them,' but they were not the solution for all men.[43]

Conclusion

At one level the politics of licensed public drinking refers to an important state-centred process. The government held a plebiscite on cocktails, appointed a commission to make recommendations as a result of the 'yes' victory, and eventually produced a new liquor act that created additional licensed facilities and slightly retooled beer parlours. If the administration of the new act did not live up to written regulations, the variations could be explained by a variety of influences: the inconsistent policies of a temperance-leaning government, pressure from interest groups, incompetence, even corruption.

To understand the varied power of regulation, however, we must consider politics also as contests over knowledge. If analysing these contests reveals anything, it is that 'truth' can be a flexible commodity indeed. For example, in the 1920s the official view was that food and entertainment promoted excessive consumption, as they were reminiscent of a saloon environment. After the Second World War the 'truth' of these amenities was that they encouraged moderation, particularly in beer parlours, where they would act as distractions from consumption. As well, before the war drys argued that public opinion could be revealed with another plebiscite on liquor. By the end of the war, as their political support continued to wane, they dismissed that option as one that would show only the extent to which the public *lacked* knowledge.

After the war, various wet groups succeeded at imposing their version of the reality of public drinking. They condemned the beer parlour as a centre of working-class excess and offered the cocktail lounge as a respectable alternative. Their success resulted in part from their ability to appropriate knowledge. They seized well-honed descriptions of beer-parlour debauchery from the drys but used them to define cocktail lounges as respectable counterpoints. Moreover, they invoked the discourse of decency for similar purposes. Public drinking was acceptable in a respectable environment – which was now the lounge. The apex of the power of wets' knowledge was the plebiscite campaign, in which 'common sense,' 'modern,' and 'citizen' dominated.

At the same time, parlour operators, workers, and some state officials contested this new understanding of public drinking. They received assistance from their unintentional allies in the temperance movement, who shifted to 'scientific discourse' to argue that adding more places to drink would not reduce drinking or attendant problems. The liquor inquiry commission set up afterwards also showed little enthusiasm for widespread licensing of lounges and cabarets, and even the newspapers acknowledged that some sort of licensed facility – ideally along the lines of British pub – had to remain in existence for working people, especially working men.

One could read the new liquor act in a number of ways. In a literal sense, beer parlours ceased to exist, replaced by 'public houses.' Yet they changed only a little. A new government bowed to what the press regarded as interest-group pressure and only tinkered with existing parlours. Moreover, hotels continued to dominate licensed public drinking. Even the press, however, admitted that hotel cocktail lounges were very different from beer parlours. Lounges emphasized a new definition of decency and public drinking, which was based on class and had its own gender distinctions and complications. Beer parlours survived, but the chronic ambivalence about them became more pronounced. They showed not only their age, but also their roots, which remained inextricably linked to the saloon, imaginary and otherwise.

Managing the Marginal

The BC beer parlour had seemed in 1925 a simple, if odd, solution to a vexing problem. As we saw in chapter 1, BC officials had sought a compromise between 'wets' and 'drys' on the issue of licensed public drinking. Even though temperance groups were unable to sustain prohibition, they had discredited the earlier saloon environment as one that nurtured indecency and undermined society. On the wet side, a loose coalition of hotels, veterans' groups, brewers, many workers, and some of their organizations lobbied for the return of at least beer by the glass. After measuring public wariness with a plebiscite, the government negotiated a deal with the hotels in 1925. Former hotel saloons legally could sell real beer as long as that was all they served. Once again people could drink in public, provided that they behaved decently. For nearly thirty years, until 1954, the beer parlour stood as the only licensed premises available to the general public. It was a coarse experiment in alcohol control, and some would call it an example of ham-fisted state regulation.

Yet one did not have to sit long (standing, after all, was not allowed) in a Vancouver parlour to realize that much more than alcohol consumption was being controlled. Because of the diversity and complexity of regulation, a simple model of social control is inadequate to explain Vancouver's beer parlours. The state and its allies were not the only regulatory actors, and regulation was not a linear process of domination and resistance. More helpful is the concept of moral regulation, which blends control and cultural approaches. 'Moral' here refers to defining and distinguishing between 'good' and 'bad.' It contains both prescriptive and proscriptive elements, but, as we saw above, 'good' and 'bad' are not fixed categories.

The analytical potential of the concept of moral regulation, however, transcends goodness, badness, and contests over them. Moral regulation renders certain types of behaviour obvious and taken for granted. For those who lean to Foucault's thoughts on governance, the potential of moral regulation is, according to Joan Sangster, that it shows 'how discourses define immorality and expert knowledge normalizes certain behaviors, producing disciplinary power that crosses the boundaries of state and civil society.' Moral regulation is closely linked to the creation of knowledge – not of fixed truths or absolutes, but of ordering and naming. Creation of knowledge is a process that involves contestation, and it is not ruled just by the powerful. This kind of analysis moves beyond the state and 'decentres' power, pushing it into Foucault's 'capillaries of society.' Rather than being the hammer of social control, moral regulation is more like a net. Power is diffused. The mesh is quite encompassing, but much gets through the holes.[1]

In the BC beer parlour, moral regulation was at work in the official knowledge of public drinking – what I have called the 'discourse of decency.' It defined moderate consumption, appropriate comportment, and heterosexual propriety. It regulated much more than alcohol – class, gender and sexuality, and the unwanted – and in practice involved a variety of actors, including those who were its objects.

From the beginning, beer parlours were conceptualized in class terms, as we saw in chapter 2, and class permeated the entire discourse of regulation – from beer as the working man's drink to behavioural expectations of patrons and workers. Because they were called workingmen's clubs, many officials, and opponents of parlours, defined them as suspect space occupied by suspect people. Supporters originally claimed that tightly regulated space would curb the excesses of working-class camaraderie. Thus regulation was both informed by class norms, received and attempted to impose different ones.

While class is fundamental to understanding parlour regulation, the way it worked undermines any simple notions of social control. Much of the regulatory burden fell on parlours' operators and workers, as we saw in chapter 2. They had the responsibility and often the power to define who was white or Indian, minor or adult, unattached or escorted, drunk or sober. Their priorities did not necessarily mesh with those of the state. Illegal singing inspired beer sales, and bookmaking had appeal for both employees and patrons. On a daily basis operators and their workers also had to consider the desires and actions of their paying customers. Patrons, after all, were not inmates. As the union handbook reminded them, waiters were to keep patrons under control, but they had to be careful not to drive away business. The regulation of violence, gambling, and the beer shortage of the Second World War highlighted many of the complexities of class and inconsistencies of regulation, including pitting parlour workers against workers as patrons.

Gender relations and sexuality also stood out prominently in beer parlours, because public drinking immediately became a site of gender contention. Liquor officials, parlour operators and staff, and many male patrons wanted for different reasons to keep public drinking for men only – the main theme of chapter 3. Some women challenged those views and were successful in expanding the boundaries of leisure. Still, decency circumscribed their behaviour, best represented by the patterns of segregated drinking and the naming of unescorted women as prostitutes. Women were condemned for illicit heterosexuality, while men were only chided. Depending on the circumstances, men and women both resisted and acquiesced in the dominant discourse. More important, their actions helped shape parlour regulation – almost literally, when one considers the installation of partitions.

A few beer parlours appealed to gay men and lesbians. The official records largely ignored their presence, which one could take as some form of toleration, perhaps best described as begrudging ignorance. Sometimes the ignorance was real, as transgendered patrons defied simple definitions of men and women. Official ire, however, was raised if gay sociability led to gay sex in parlour washrooms. Finally, the social space for lesbians was more restricted than that for gay men. Lesbians were confined largely to the rougher, skid-road facilities. Gay men had more options, but, then, they were men.

Beer parlour decency also defined and regulated those who were unwanted. It is probably necessary but certainly not sufficient to note that adult, white, Anglo-Celtic heterosexual men were the standard by which others were judged. The unwanted – especially the mixed-raced couples, Asians, minors, and status Indians that we considered in chapter 4 – were real people, but they were also categories of concern complicated by appearance and behaviour. For example, in Vancouver's parlours the regulation of Aboriginal people and of minors was closely linked. Both were barred by statute; Indians, however, were permanent wards of the state, while minors eventually grew up. Some minors and Aboriginal people used appearance and behaviour to shed, temporarily, their status as illegals. Just as important, 'minor' and 'Indian' proved to be flexible categories of regulation. Even after Aboriginal people were allowed in parlours, the 'beer parlour Indian' did not disappear.

In the other direction, a mixed-race couple disappeared if it did not include a man of colour and a white woman. That combination 'racialized' both people and potentially destabilized the category 'white' through some people's fears of miscegenation. Race thus included the dominance of white heterosexual men over women and other men of colour. Asians, especially Chinese, were defined in part by their alleged historic links to vice. Such definitions had real regulatory impact, as one of the indicators of parlours' decency was their lack of Asian operators or workers.

By the end of the Second World War, both wets and drys agreed that regulation of beer parlours had done little to enhance the respectability of the facilities or their patrons. Some went further and argued that parlours promoted the excesses that they were supposed to curtail. While wets were not of one mind, their views dominated public discourse. What emerged after the war (chapter 5) was a new 'knowledge' of public drinking, which linked decency to different venues of drinking, especially cocktail lounges that catered to middle-class drinkers. Cocktail supporters argued that lounges and their patrons would be more respectable and need less regulation than parlours and their patrons.

In the early 1950s beer parlours withstood the effects of a plebiscite, a commission of inquiry, and legislative changes that produced more licensed facilities, including cocktail lounges. In a slightly altered form the parlours remained working-class facilities, and their regulation continued to be contentious. Though heavily patronized, they became more morally marginalized.

Carolyn Strange and Tina Loo describe moral regulation as 'a way of managing the marginal, whether that marginality was conferred by race, class, or gender.' While individuals' behaviour was important, it was so because it categorized them. Much of the power of regulation derived from its defining of people and space, and regulation was closely linked to status and place. An unescorted woman buying milk in a food market provoked different regulatory definitions than the same woman who entered a beer parlour by herself. Wage workers who drank in beer parlours did not necessarily consume more alcohol than their middle-class counterparts in cocktail lounges. Yet because of who they were and where they drank, they received more regulatory attention. Take, for instance, two working-class men who knew about martinis, put them in suits and a cocktail lounge, and they could pass as professionals.[2]

Most of the regulatory initiative came from state officials, but Strange and Loo emphasize that state success was often less than spectacular. The 'lofty goals and high hopes' were well-nigh impossible to achieve, and regulation often 'failed by its own standards.' Moreover, regulation was expensive, complex, and time consuming. In the end, negotiating morality often proved to be cheaper and easier than eliminating vice.[3]

By both design and accident, depending on the circumstances, regulatory targets were not clear. On the one hand, for example, health officials claimed that their main interest was retarding the spread of venereal disease, but they ended up defining appropriate sexuality for women in general. On the other hand, the ban on food and entertainment in beer parlours was seriously intended to deflate saloon ambience and inhibit consumption. Legally, however, there was little to do in a Vancouver parlour but drink. Finally, of course, regulation met much resistance from those regulated, who acted according to their own views and often derailed official regulation.

Indeed, regulation of beer parlours in Vancouver was a more complex process than a linear model of social control dominated by the state can reveal. Regulation involved a number of actors and operated at different levels simultaneously. The state did not control all these facets, and state officials were not necessarily even aware of all the combinations and permutations of regulation.

Still, one must conclude that the state remained a powerful manager of the marginal, for at least four reasons. First, and most generally, parlours existed within capitalistic economic relations. Most state theorists long ago abandoned the idea that the state acts at the behest of capital. Rather, the state acts on behalf of capital – that is, it defends the long-term interests of capital. In order to do so, the state needs a fair amount of autonomy. The relative autonomy of the state – its the ability to regulate – helps 'save the bourgeoisie from itself.' State regulation seeks to attenuate class conflict, facilitate accumulation, and enhance legitimacy – of the state and capitalism. Obviously capitalism in Canada did not rest on the success, failure, or even existence of Vancouver's beer parlours. Yet if a regulatory state did not exist, capital would have to invent it.[4]

Second, state regulation did not have to be completely successful. Although the records often suggest that the parlour was bedlam born of beer, we should not dismiss the impact of state regulation. Orderly parlours, where patrons sat where they should and with whom they should, drank moderate amounts of beer, and acted as expected, simply did not warrant much comment.

We can read the silence as a measure of decency's achievement. Well-behaved patrons could be construed as regulation by internalization, or government of the self. The state could not control this process, but internalization upheld its values and enhanced legitimacy. While internalization was the ideal, the state required only acquiescence to achieve many objectives. No doubt in many cases state officials conflated acquiescence with internalization. Yet from an inspector's point of view, the more important feature of a quiet parlour was that it required less paperwork, which was close enough to the lofty goals of regulation.

At the same time, however, we should not confuse acquiescence with consent. As Philip Corrigan and Derek Sayer argue, compliance does not always mean incorporation or internalization. A collective response is not necessarily a unitary one. People may act the same way for a variety of motives. Mark Leier goes a step farther. He maintains that whenever the threat or reality of 'unpleasant consequences' exists, 'whether these be overt or implied, material or psychological, it is impossible to distinguish between consent and coercion.' Coercion operates both formally and informally, and what passes for consent 'may be manipulated in a number of ways.' Reward and punishment are two sides of the same coin. Leier's intention is to show that 'all authority is illegitimate,' but his argument reveals some of the subtleties of coercion.[5]

Third, coercion helps explain the power of the state. While liberal states have developed a variety of means to negotiate what appears to be consent, the state still has a monopoly on the legitimate use of force. In Vancouver's beer parlours the state's authority was fragmented, and the outcomes of regulation were not necessarily predictable, consistent, or even the ones sought. Still, regulation was not a process that engaged equals on a 'level playing field.' The state could draw on a variety of coercive resources. Officials arrested people, had them barred or fired, and ruined reputations. Parlour operators had their licences suspended or cancelled. In general, Foucault was wise to shift our gaze away from power as state-centred repression. Certainly the state risks losing its legitimacy if it resorts to coercion too often or too intensely. Yet state coercion used judiciously and creatively is an effective means of regulation.[6]

Finally, the state remained a powerful regulator because it also produced knowledge. The state ordered reality and made truth. For example, in Vancouver the state defined drinking space as public or private, prescribing different forms of regulation. Certainly the state did not initiate or even control all of this regulation. It did not offer 'memberships' in private clubs or mandate the purchase of 'set-ups' in cabarets. Yet it named the space that allowed different forms of regulation and regulators to flourish.

State knowledge also permeated racial regulation. In her study of Vancouver's Chinatown, Kay Anderson, relying on Edward Said, argues that 'social reality is constructed not democratically but within a hegemonic framework that is rarely questioned.' She concludes that 'politicians and bureaucrats' used their 'moral and legal authority' to 'give the race concept its remarkable material force and effect, embedding it in structures that over time reciprocally reproduced it.' In beer parlours, state officials reinforced dominant racial standards. Their lack of consistency, in both promotion and success, should not obviate the significance of the standards that they accepted.[7]

A more vivid example of the state as producer of knowledge comes from the BC liquor commission of inquiry in 1952. Peta Sheriff argues that such commissions are 'part of the legitimation function of the state such that their contribution to policy formation is less important than is their contribution to social harmony.' Moreover, Adam Ashforth describes such bodies as theatres of power that are fundamental to the legitimation of the state. They 'produce a discourse celebrating a marriage of truth and power in the modern State through rational identification of a purportedly objective Common Good.' They transform 'contentious matters of political struggle into discourses of reasoned argument.' They create the 'truth' that a common good exists to be discovered. Thus, even when a commission appears to undermine the state, as here by finding evidence of liquor corruption and patronage, it upholds the legitimacy of the state. Exposing corruption is part of the discovery of the common good.[8]

Understanding the state requires going beyond looking at structures and institutions to examine processes. Colin Hay argues that the state is a 'constantly changing network of relationships and institutional practices and procedures.' The state is not an object, but rather a process of rule embedded in material relations. From this vantage one attributes a single mentality neither to the state nor to its institutions. Philip Corrigan and Derek Sayer emphasize the point that the power of the state is not just external and objective, but also internal and subjective. The state 'works through us.' It helps to organize individual and collective representations. The results are not necessarily consistent, but the effects help keep the state a powerful regulator, as we see in this book, in Vancouver's beer parlours.[9]

Notes

Introduction: Regulating Public Drinking

1 Despite the title of Cheryl Krasnick Warsh's collection, *Drink in Canada*, the majority of the articles focus on temperance subjects. The same is true, of course, of Jan Noel's award-winning *Canada Dry*. As for Sharon Cook's study of the Ontario Woman's Christian Temperance Union (WCTU), it is a work on evangelicalism as much as on temperance; see Cook, 'Through Sunshine and Shadow.' *The Changing Face of Drink*, edited by Jack Blocker and Cheryl Warsh, is more diverse. Yet in the three articles there devoted to Canada, temperance is a major theme in two of them. Paradoxically, however, we do not have a recent Canadian history of prohibition. The standard, very sympathetic, work remains Spence, *Prohibition in Canada*.

2 See Gray, *Booze*, 52–68, 205–10, and Gray, *Bacchanalia Revisited*, chaps. 3 and 4.

3 Jack Blocker, 'Introduction,' in Blocker and Warsh, eds., *The Changing Face of Drink*, 1 (quotation), 5, 10.

4 Susanna Barrows and Robin Room, 'Introduction,' in Barrows and Room, eds., *Drinking*, 7–8; Pope, 'Fish into Wine,' 269–71.

5 The idea of poor man's club or workingman's club is at the heart of Powers, *Faces along the Bar*. She argues that both friends and foes of the saloon used the phrases; see 13. See also Kingsdale, 'The "Poor Man's Club."' Two Canadian works that fit well with the concept of the workingman's club are DeLottinville, 'Joe Beef of Montreal,' and Christie, 'The Function of the Tavern.'

6 Powers, *Faces along the Bar*, 28 (1st quotation), 34, 94 (2nd quotation), 106; Brennan, *Public Drinking*, 14; Rosenzweig, *Eight Hours*, 40–59. See also Prothero, *Radical Artisans*, 285–6; Haine, *The World of the Parisian Cafe*; Thompson,

Rum Punch and Revolution. Peter DeLottinville refers to Joe Beef's Canteen in Montreal as a 'male bastion,' although his sources make some references to prostitution. See 'Joe Beef of Montreal,' 17 n24 (quotation) and 10 n2.

7 Hey, *Patriarchy*, 69–70 (quotation on 69). See also Cheryl Krasnick Warsh, '"Oh, Lord, pour a cordial in her wounded heart": The Drinking Woman in Victorian and Edwardian Canada,' in Warsh, ed., *Drink in Canada*, 85; Leigh, '"A thing so fallen"'; Park, 'Only "Those Women"'; Ahlstrom, 'Cultural Differences.' In a manner similar to Hey, Dimitra Gefou-Madianou has argued that male public drinking in contemporary Euro-Mediterranean societies represents an anti-domestic discourse. The exclusion of women reinforces female subordination and obscures male dependence on women. Public drinking camaraderie helps to construct heterosexual masculine identity and allows men to transcend their everyday roles and domestic responsibilities. See Gefou-Madianou, 'Introduction: Alcohol, Commensality, Identity Transformations and Transcendence,' in Gefou-Madianou, ed., *Alcohol*, 8, 13.

8 Clark, *The English Alehouse*, 21–2, 205–6; Bennett, 'The Village Ale-Wife'; Bennett, *Ale, Beer and Brewsters*; Padmavathy, 'The English Barmaid'; Bailey, 'Parasexuality and Glamour.' In Australia women were banned from public bars, but they were also employed as barmaids. See Kirkby, *Barmaids*.

9 Conroy, *In Public Houses*, 103–9; McBurney and Byers, *Tavern in the Town*, 12; Guillet, *Pioneer Inns and Taverns*, Vol. 2, Part 4, 152.

10 Powers, *Faces along the Bar*, 35. Catherine Gilbert Murdock does not question that 'the saloon and similar organizations were exclusive male spaces.' Yet her work does emphasize the complexities of gender and drink. See *Domesticating*, quote at 14.

11 Duis, *The Saloon*, 2–6, 252–3, 265, 276–7.

12 Powers, *Faces along the Bar*, 33–5 (quotation on 33); see also Duis, *The Saloon*, 106.

13 Judith Fingard, *The Dark Side*, 121–2; Fingard, '"A Great Big Rum Shop,"' 93–6.

14 Peiss, *Cheap Amusements*, 28; Rosenzweig, *Eight Hours*, 183; Gutzke, 'Gender, Class, and Public Drinking,' 368–9.

15 Gutzke, 'Gender, Class and Public Drinking,' 382–3, 388–9; Peiss, *Cheap Amusements*, 28; Mary Murphy, *Mining Cultures*, 43. See also Peter Clark, *The English Alehouse*, 235–6; Tlusty, 'Gender and Alcohol Use.'

16 Warsh, '"Oh, Lord, pour a cordial,"' in Warsh, ed., *Drink in Canada*, 75–6 (quotation on 76); British Columbia, *Revised Statutes of British Columbia*, 1911, s. 65. Vancouver city banned women from its saloons in 1909.

17 Blocker, 'Introduction,' in Blocker and Warsh, eds., *The Changing Face of*

Drink, 5–6. See also Prestwich, 'The Regulation of Drinking,' 369–71; Gareth Stedman Jones, 'Class Expressionism.'

18 Franca Iacovetta and Mariana Valverde, 'Introduction,' in Iacovetta and Valverde, eds., *Gender Conflicts*, xviii; Frader, 'Dissent over Discourse.' On the debates over class closer to home see *BC Studies* 111 (autumn 1996), which has a forum on class and the writing of BC history. In the leading piece and final comment, Mark Leier strongly defends class as the fundamental analytical perspective. Bryan D. Palmer, Robert A.J. McDonald, and Veronica Strong-Boag offer responses.

19 The classic poststructuralist text is Joan Scott's collection of essays, *Gender and the Politics of History*, but more useful for the Canadian context are Joy Parr, 'Gender History,' and Tina Loo, *Making Law*, 7 (quotation). The standard critique of poststructuralism is Palmer, *Descent into Discourse*, which he updated in 'Critical Theory.' Though not disappointed to see class fall from grace, Christopher Kent has written one of the clearest summaries of the debates of the last two decades; see his 'Victorian Social History.'

20 Frader, 'Dissent over Discourse,' 216, 230 (1st 2 quotations); Canning, *Languages of Labor and Gender*, 10–14 (quotation on 14). See also Strange, *Toronto's Girl Problem*, 11–12; Marks, *Revivals and Roller Rinks*, especially 8–10.

21 Dean, '"A social structure of many souls,"' 158 (quoting Foucault); Sangster, 'Incarcerating "Bad Girls,"' 241; Adams, 'In Sickness and in Health,' 119; see also Michel Foucault, 'Governmentality,' 102–3; Corrigan and Sayer, *The Great Arch*, 4. Another stream of literature on moral regulation winds its way back to Karl Marx, usually via Antonio Gramsci's concept of hegemony. Mariana Valverde has argued that Marxian and Foucaultian approaches to moral regulation share much 'political common ground' because they both focus on 'power and domination.' See Mariana Valverde, 'Editor's Introduction,' *Canadian Journal of Sociology* 19 (1994), vi–vii (quotations).

22 Foucault, *Power/Knowledge*, 96–7, 119, 133; Scott, *Gender*, 2. Foucault discussed his conceptions of power in *The History of Sexuality*, Vol. 1, *An Introduction*, 92–102.

1: The Genesis of the Beer Parlour

1 Albert John Hiebert, 'Prohibition,' 16.

2 Ibid., 15–16; McDonald, *Making Vancouver*, 13; Betty Keller, *On the Shady Side*, 3–6.

3 The material in this paragraph and the next ten derives largely from my *Demon Rum*, chap. 1.

4 On the dilemma of revenue versus control see my '"Profit was just a circumstance."'

5 Congdon to Manson, 30 Dec. 1924, British Columbia Archives (BCA), Victoria, GR1323, B2204; Weldon to Premier, 18 Oct. 1922, GR1323, B2199.

6 Campbell to Manson, 31 Dec. 1924, BCA, GR1323, B2204; Kenneth Campbell, 'A Tribute to Pioneer Members ...,' *British Columbia Hotelman* 20 (Sept.–Oct. 1958); 6, 8; British Columbia, *Statutes*, 1947, c. 53, s. 11. I calculated the separate room leases from BCA, GR52, which contains LCB Inspector files.

7 On the working world of Vancouver, see Robert A.J. McDonald, 'Working,' 25–33; Peter Trower, *Deadman's Ticket*, 27.

8 Marquis, 'Vancouver Vice,' 267.

9 Groth, *Living Downtown*, 23, 204–28.

10 Adams, '"Almost anything can happen,"' 218 (quotation); Valverde, *Diseases of the Will*, 12, 144 (quotation). See also Blomley, 'Text and Context,' 516–18, 520–1.

11 Valverde, *Diseases of the Will*, 153–4.

12 British Columbia, *Statutes*, 1921, c. 30, s. 45; Government Liquor Act Amendment Act, 1933, s. 51; *Revised Statutes*, 1924, c. 146, ss. 4, 8, 9. Davidson to Manson, 1 Dec. 1927, BCA, GR1323, B2302 (bottled versus draft beer).

13 The original regulations for beer parlours appeared in *Fourth Annual Report of the Liquor Control Board of the Province of British Columbia (Fourth AR LCB)* (1925), J64–7.

14 I discuss partitions in beer parlours and their influence on regulation in much greater detail below in chapter 3. On the ban against female parlour workers, see ibid., J66.

15 Kennedy to Norgan, 25 April 1949, BCA GR52, Box 8, File 121–319.

16 Robert A. Campbell, *Demon Rum*, 80, 122, 129. On liquor corruption in British Columbia see ibid., 97–102, and my 'Liquor and Liberals.'

17 In 1929 chartered accountant Albert Griffiths completed a report on liquor for the newly elected Conservative government. He concluded that only one of three inspectors had 'the faintest idea of his duties and responsibilities.' See 'Report of Investigations and Inquiries in Connection with the Administration of the Liquor Control Board,' 31 Dec. 1929, p. 4, BCA, GR1323, B2307.

18 While a rich source, the files emphasize the post-1945 period. In the late 1940s one parlour operator claimed that when John Haywood became chief inspector in 1947 he burned the old files. The claim cannot be substantiated, but if he did, fortunately he did not get everything. See the

anonymous report to Harold Winch, Jan. 194_ [sic], University of British Columbia, Special Collections, Angus MacInnis Memorial Collection, Box 41a, File 9, 30.

19 George Chauncey, *Gay New York*, 337; Valverde, *Diseases of the Will*, 150–3.

2: Operators and Workers: The Ties That Bind

1 University of British Columbia (UBC), Special Collections (SC), Hotel, Restaurant Culinary Employees and Bartenders Union, Local 40 (HRCEBU), Box 6, *Official Handbook, 1950–1951*, 3 (quotation), 53–4; Box 6, Minute Book, May 1937–Dec. 1957: 7 Dec. 1949.

2 UBC, SC, Vancouver and District Labour Council (V&DLC), Minute Book 1923–1926: 5 May 1925, 2 June 1925, 1 Sept. 1925. The reference to Hanafin helping to keep the union alive comes from UBC, SC, HRCEBU, Box 6, *Official Handbook, 1949–50*, 8–9. See also City of Vancouver Archives (CVA), Hotel, Restaurant and Culinary Employees and Bartenders Union, Local 40 (HRCEBU), Add. Mss. 723, Vol. 1, File 7, 'Outstanding and Fiery Unionist Supported Our Amalgamation,' [c. 1974]. The spelling of 'Hanafin' varies, but that is how he signed his name.

  The international union – an affiliate of the American Federation of Labor (AFL) – was chartered in 1891 with 450 members. Since 1981 it has been called Hotel Employees and Restaurant Employees (HERE). See Dorothy Sue Cobble, *Dishing It Out*, 61, 249 n5.

3 Campbell, *Demon Rum*, 23; UBC, SC, HRCEBU, Box 4, Minute Book, July 1914–Dec. 1918: 17 April 1918, 23 July 1918.

4 *Province*, 28 July 1934, 31; Kennedy to Maitland, 3 June 1942, Records Management Branch (RMB), Attorney General Files (AG), Reel 618; 'Minimum Scale of Wages of the Beer Parlors,' BCA, GR770, Box 5, File 199. Some hotels employed 'combination' workers who both pulled and served beer.

5 On pushing beer, see Bruce to Director, 18 April 1953, BCA, GR52, Box 9, File 121-362; *Fourth AR LCB* (1925), J67 (tips).

6 John M. Rienstra, an economist for Joseph P. Ward & Associates, prepared the consultant's report submitted 19 June 1957, see RMB, AG, Reel 509, 7–8 (quotation on 7); tray weights, Local 676 to McGugan, 9 July 1952, RMB, AG, Reel 371, File L217-2, 1951.

7 For a good description of how dispatching worked, see the minutes of the meeting of 31 October 1954 of Local 676, in UBC, SC, Box 6, Minute Book, May 1952–Feb. 1955. One man worked at sixteen hotels in four years before he got a steady job at the Manitoba Hotel. See BCA, GR52, Box 9, File 121-342.

8 Brief Submitted to Conciliation Board Hearing Re Local 676 by the British Columbia Hotels Association, 18 May 1953, CVA, HRCEBU, Vol. 2, File 1 (1st and 2nd quotations); BCHA to Members, 24 Sept. 1937, BCA GR770, Box 5, File 199; Hume to Haywood, 4 July 1951, GR52, Box 7, File 121-321 (3rd quotation).

9 Mills to Haywood, 18 Aug. 1948, BCA, GR52, Box 9, File 121–357; Haywood to Mills, 19 Aug. 1948, ibid. (quotation).

10 See UBC, SC, HRCEBU, box 1, Minute Book, Jan. 1955–July 1964: 30 Aug. 1955, 8 Jan. 1957, 8 Dec. 1957, 14 March 1958, and 27 Aug. 1958; 'Rules of Registration of Beverage Dispensers Union, Local 676, n.d. [1958?], CVA, HRCEBU, Vol. 2, File 2 (1st quotation); Bonner to McGugan, 31 Aug. 1965, RMB, AG, Reel 617 (2nd quotation).

11 On Rose Low, see BCA, GR770, Box 13, File 2; 1935 BCHA letterhead, ibid., Box 5, File 199; *Province*, 23 Feb. 1940, 11; on Mary Rosen, see BCA, GR48, Box 15, File 2; on Europe Hotel, see 1948 Inspector's Hotel Report, GR52, Box 8, File 121-330. The sources for the references to directors, owners, and room managers are BCA, GR-2, LCB, Inspector Files. Six hotels had women listed as owners or co-owners, and five had them as room managers.

12 'Brief submitted on behalf of: Beverage Dispensers Local 676 ...,' CVA, HRCEBU, Vol. 2, File 1, p. 6; on women servers in interior hotels, see, for example, Skeena Hotel (Terrace), BCA, GR52, Box 7, File 12-294; Grandview Hotel (South Hazelton), ibid., File 121-293; New Lytton Hotel (Lytton), ibid., File 121-301.

13 See Inspector Files (BCA, GR52) for Manitoba, Dufferin, Lotus, New Empire, Dominion, Kingston, Pacific, and Ivanhoe Hotels. On Galloway, see Haywood to Chief Constable, 30 April 1952, GR52, Box 8, File 121-327; UBC, SC, HRCEBU, Box 6, Minute Book, May 1952–Feb. 1955: 30 Nov. 1952; Box 1, Minute Book, Jan. 1955–July 1964: 8 Dec. 1957, 30 June 1963; Box 7, Minute Book, Jan. 1958–Jan. 1974: 1962 minutes, passim.

14 Beddome to McGugan, 3 Aug. 1953, BCA, GR52, Box 8, File 121-327 (quotation).

15 Brandolini to Haywood, 24 April 1953, ibid., File 121-329; Chester to LCB, 10 Feb. 1936, GR1323, B2308.

16 [Agent] to Chief Inspector, 3 Feb. 1952, BCA, GR52, Box 9, File 121-359 (quotations); Pettit to Supervisor, 6 Feb. 1952, ibid. On the VCW's concern about bus fares, see UBC, SC, Vancouver Council of Women (VCW), Box 9, File 4, Committee of Officers Meeting, 24 Aug. 1954.

17 Miller to Hose, 8 Feb. 1928, BCA, GR770, Box 12, File 12; Bruce to Director, 15 Dec. 1952, GR52, Box 8, File 121-326.

18 Lythgoe to Chief Inspector, 24 June 1951, BCA, GR52, Box 9, File 121-349 (New Fountain); see also Chief Inspector to Chairman, 15 Jan. 1949, GR52, Box 9, File 121-366.
19 Chief Inspector to Chairman, 27 March 1951, BCA, GR52, Box 8, File 121-327.
20 Ibid. (quotations); Secretary to Dominion Holdings, 28 March 1951, ibid.; BCHA notice is from BCA, GR770, Box 5, File 199. For other examples of singing, see the list of notations for the Yale Hotel (GR52, Box 9, File 121–367), the West Hotel (Box 9, File 121-366), the Anchor Hotel (Box 7, File 121-310), and the Marr Hotel (Box 8, File 121-335). Music initially caught the authorities off guard. The original regulations banned only games, sports, and dancing. Music and musical instruments were explicitly prohibited the next year. See *Fourth AR LCB* (1925), J67 and *Fifth AR LCB* (1926), O67. On pub singing as a form of popular radicalism, see Prothero, *Radical Artisans*, 290–8.
21 Vancouver *Sun*, 20 June 1952 (1st quotation); *News-Herald*, 21 June 1952; Pettit to Director, 20 June 1952, BCA, GR52, Box 7, File 121-316 (2nd quotation). On other investigations sparked by newspaper accounts, see, for example, Pettit to Supervisor, 29 May 1952, Box 9, File 121-364; Bruce to Director, 7 April 1953, Box 8, File 121-340.
22 Chief Constable to Chief Inspector, 7 July 1948, and list of notations, BCA, GR52, Box 8, File 121–329 (New Empire); list of notations for St Regis, Box 9, File 121-360. See also list of notations for Stanley, Box 9, File 121-362.
23 [Agent] to Chief Inspector, 15 March 1949, BCA, GR52, Box 9, File 121-366 (bloody nose); Bruce to Director, 18 Aug. 1953, ibid., Box 7, File 121-310 (Anchor).
24 Pettit to Director, 4 Aug. 1952, ibid., Box 8, File 121-323 (Columbia); Bruce to Director, 7 Oct. 1952, Box 9, File 121-362 (Stanley).
25 Bruce to Director, 7 April 1953, ibid., Box 8, File 121-340.
26 'Brief submitted on behalf of: Beverage Dispensers Local 676 ...,' CVA, HRCEBU, Vol. 2, File 1, p. 2 (quotation); Bruce to Director, 29 Oct. 1952, BCA, GR52, Box 9, File 121-355.
27 UBC, SC, HRCEBU, Box 6, *Official Handbook, 1949–1950*, 31.
28 Marquis, 'Vancouver Vice,' 246–7.
29 Haywood to Mulligan, 22 Nov. 1948, BCA, GR52, Box 8, File 121-329.
30 Macdonald and O'Keefe, *The Mulligan Affair*, 11–14, 129–30.
31 Corbett to Secretary, 3 Sept. 1946, BCA, GR52, Box 8, File 121-340 (quotations); Haywood to Chairman, 24 Sept. 1952, ibid.
32 Newspaper clippings, 7 July 1951, ibid., File 121-340; Haywood to Chairman, 24 Sept. 1952, ibid. (quotation).

33 See list of notations, Abbotsford Hotel, ibid., Box 7, File 121-307; R. to LCB, 11 Sept. 1950, ibid., Box 9, File 121-358 (1st quotation); Kimberly to Chief Inspector, 18 Sept. 1950, ibid. (2nd quotation).

34 While race – in the form of the historic association of Chinese with gambling – may have provided a subtext, the LCB had other, more explicit concerns about maintaining its regulatory authority. See chapter 4 below.

35 *Province*, 14 May 1940, 18 (1st quotation); Thorson to Hart, 12 Jan. 1942, RMB, AG, Reel 371 (2nd quotation); *Province*, 24 Sept. 1942, 3 (polls), 17 Dec. 1942, 8. The VCW, led by the WCTU, launched its campaign against liquor and public drinking almost as the war began. See, for example, UBC, SC, VCW, Box 8, File 3 (2 Oct. 1939), and File 5 (5 May 1941).

36 BCHA to Attorney General, 3 Oct. 1942, BCA, GR770, Box 5, File 199; Hotel Association of Canada to L.R. LaFleche, 26 Oct. 1942, ibid.

37 *Province*, 23 Dec. 1942, 11 (poll), 28 Nov. 1942, 1–2 (rationing); Kennedy to McIntyre, 3 Dec. 1942, BCA, GR770, Box 2, File 126-1 (quotation); Kennedy to Belton, 23 Feb. 1943, ibid., Box 4, File 162; 'Various Steps Taken – Restrictions on Sale of Liquor,' ibid.

38 Kennedy to Belton, 23 Feb. 1943, BCA, GR770, Box 4, File 162; UBC, SC, V&DLC, Minute Book 1940–1946: 16 Feb. 1943 (1st quotation), 2 March 1943 (2nd quotation), 6 April 1943.

39 UBC, SC, International Union of Mine, Mill and Smelter Workers (Canada), Box 6, Folder 3, Resolution 233; Victoria *Colonist*, 15 Jan. 1944.

40 Robert A. Campbell, *Demon Rum*, 86–7 (price increases); UBC, SC, V&DLC, Minute Book 1940–1946: 16 March 1943; Kennedy to Sloan, 2 Aug. 1934, BCA, GR1323, B2311; Neely to Bonner, 7 Oct. 1957, RMB, AG, Reel 449.

41 UBC, SC, V&DLC, Minute Book 1940–1946: 16 March 1943, 20 July 1943 (1st quotation), 21 Sept. 1943; Kahn to Members, 12 April 1944, BCA, GR770, Box 5, File 199 (2nd quotation); Kennedy to Brazier, 29 May 1944, ibid. (3rd quotation).

42 Kahn to Members, 10 June 1944, BCA, GR770, Box 5, File 199 (1st and 2nd quotations); Kahn to Members, 27 June 1944, ibid. (3rd quotation).

43 Kennedy to Maitland, 19 Feb. 1946, RMB, AG, Reel 371; *Colonist*, 6 April 1946; BCHA to Bonner, 5 Dec. 1953, RMB, AG, Reel 449. Samuel Plimsoll was a Yorkshire brewery manager who, as an MP for Derby in the 1870s, was credited with the regulation that required merchant ships to have clearly marked limit lines on the hull to prevent – ironically, in the context of beer – overloading. See 'Samuel Plimsoll, M.P.,' *The Plimsoll Club*. <http://www.plimsoll.com/history.html> (5 Jan. 2000).

44 This paragraph was inspired in part by Ava Baron, 'On Looking at Men:

Masculinity and the Making of a Gendered Working-Class History,'
especially 157–8; Mackenzie to Bonner, 28 Aug. 1953, RMB, AG, Reel 449
(quotation); UBC, SC, HRCEBU, Box 6, *Official Handbook, 1950–1951,* 15;
see also *Province,* 18 Aug. 1967, 19.

45 British Columbia Liquor Control and Licensing Branch, Victoria, Minutes
of the Liquor Control Board of British Columbia (LCB Minutes), Vol. 23
(1944), 661. On coercion of operators, see the letter from a former parlour
worker to the attorney general, 14 Oct. 1959, RMB, AG, Reel 449.

46 Thomas Dunk, *It's a Working-Man's Town,* 38 (1st quotation), 153, 160 (2nd
quotation).

3: Ladies and Escorts: Regulating and Negotiating Gender and Sexuality

1 *Vancouver Daily Province,* 31 May 1925, 1; LCB, 'Circular Letter No. 172,'
12 June 1925, BCA, GR770, Box 5, File 199B.

2 Strong-Boag, *The New Day Recalled,* 41; Barman, *The West beyond the West,*
243–4; Strange, *Toronto's Girl Problem,* 10, 17. On the development of
heterosocial leisure see Peiss, *Cheap Amusements,* especially chaps. 1 and 3.

3 James H. Gray, *The Roar of the Twenties,* 195; *Sun,* 16 June 1984, A16; *Fourth
AR LCB* (1925), J64–7.

4 *Province,* 6 May 1925 (1st quotation); 'Memorandum for The Hon. Attorney General,' 8 May 1925, BCA, GR1323, B2308 (2nd quotation); *Province,*
21 May 1925, 1.

5 *Province,* 28 April 1926, 1, 23 July 1926, 7, 26 March 1926, 6 (editorial).

6 Ibid., 30 July 1926, 1, 29 July 1926, 1 (quotations); *Sun,* 31 July 1926, in LCB
Scrapbooks, Vol. 20, BCA, GR62 (editorial).

7 *Province,* 30 July 1926, 24.

8 *Province,* 23 July 1926, 7; *Victoria Times,* 30 July 1926, in LCB Scrapbooks,
Vol. 20.

9 *Sun,* 16 Aug. 1926, LCB Scrapbooks, Vol. 20; Tuley to Sutherland, 26 May
1927, BCA, GR1323, B2309 (1st quotation); *Province,* 27 May 1927, LCB
Scrapbooks, Vol. 20 (2nd quotation); Tysoe to Attorney General, 22 June
1927, BCA, GR1323, B2309; *Province,* 6 July 1927, 28, 7 July 1927, 1; 'Government Liquor Act – Suggested amendment of section 27, [1927],'
GR1323, B2308.

10 Secretary to Brewster, 16 May 1917, UBC, SC, VCW, Box 1, File 1; see also
Secretary to Stevens, 30 June 1919, Box 1, File 2. On the class and ideologi-
cal makeup of the VCW, see Rose, '"Keepers of Morale,"' and Weiss, '"As
Women and as Citizens."' See also Weiss, 'The Brightest Women,' 199–209.
On the National Council of Women of Canada, see Griffiths, *The Splendid*

Vision. It is helpful to read *The Splendid Vision*, a commissioned history, while consulting Strong-Boag's more critical *The Parliament of Women.*

11 Sub-executive resolution, 7 March 1921, UBC, SC, VCW, Box 6, File 7 (1st quotation); general resolution, 2 June 1924, ibid., Box 6, File 8 (2nd quotation).

12 *Province*, 31 Oct. 1926, 12.

13 Ibid., editorial, 29 July 1926, 6, 8 Aug. 1926, Magazine Section, 8 (Hurt).

14 Secretary to Davidson, 7 Aug. 1930, BCA, GR770, Box 2, File 109.

15 Valverde, '"When the Mother of the Race Is Free,"' 3–6; Bacchi, 'Race Regeneration and Social Purity,' 315–16; Cassel, *The Secret Plague*, 20 (quotation). See also Valverde, *The Age of Light, Soap, and Water*, 77–9.

16 Cassel, *The Secret Plague*, 123, 128–31; Buckley and McGinnis, 'Venereal Disease,' 338–9.

17 Cassel, *The Secret Plague*, 169, 200; British Columbia, *Statutes*, 1919, c. 88, 3, 11.

18 Cassel, *The Secret Plague*, 169, 190–1, 200; Buckley and McGinnis, 'Venereal Disease,' 347–9. See also Adams, 'In Sickness and in Health,' 117–30.

19 Cassel, *The Secret Plague*, 200–1; Freund, 'The Politics of Naming,' 39; *Province*, 19 March 1938, 6; Williams, 'Commercialized Prostitution,' 465 (quotation), 466.

20 Kahn to Kennedy, 22 Feb. 1937, BCA, GR770, Box 5, File 199.

21 *Province*, 12 Jan. 1939, 5 (Board of Trade); Kennedy to Wismer, 27 Jan. 1939, ibid.

22 Williams to Kahn, 7 March 1939, ibid., File 199B.

23 Kahn to Senior, 6 October 1939, ibid.

24 Kennedy to Angelus Holding Company, 13 Jan. 1941, ibid. (1st quotation); Williams to Wismer, 8 April 1942, ibid., File 199A (2nd quotation).

25 'Partitions in Beer Parlours,' 23 April 1942, ibid., File 199A; Kennedy to Blackwell, 13 Dec. 1944, ibid., File 199B; Galvin to Kennedy, 15 June 1942, ibid., File 199A.

26 Cleveland to Kennedy, 9 December 1942, (quotations), ibid., File 199A; Saxton to Kennedy, 13 November 1943, ibid., File 199B.

27 'V.D. Infections Allegedly Acquired from Persons Met in Beer Parlours, 1939–1944,' ibid., File 199B; *Vancouver News-Herald*, 15 Oct. 1942, 9.

28 Kennedy to Saxton, 29 April 1944, BCA, GR770, Box 5, File 199B.

29 Cassel, *The Secret Plague*, 11, 58; Kennedy to Elliot, 3 Oct. 1947, ibid., File 199A; Elliot to Kennedy, 21 Nov. 1947, ibid.; 'Minutes of the Quarterly Facilitation Meeting, 18 November 1949,' ibid.

30 British Columbia, *Statutes*, 1947, c. 95, s. 8; 'Minutes of the Facilitation Meeting,' BCA, GR770, Box 5, File 199A, [1948] (examination centre).

31 Inspector to Hose, 7 Feb. 1928, BCA, GR770, Box 12, File 4 (1st quotation) and c. 1928 blueprint for Grand Union; Chief Inspector to Secretary, 20 Nov. 1931, Box 13, File 2 (2nd quotation); Chief Inspector to Empire Hotel, 20 Nov. 1931, ibid. (3rd quotation).

32 Wyllie to Sir, 23 April 1942, ibid., Box 5, File 199A; Wyllie to Chief Inspector, 30 April 1948, GR52, Box 9, File 121–355.

33 British Columbia, *Statutes*, 1947, c. 53, s. 11; *28th AR LCB* (1949), 9. See, for example, Kimberly to Chief Inspector, 12 Nov. 1949, BCA, GR52, Box 8, File 121–337 (partitions, Ivanhoe Hotel); Columbia Hotel, list of notations (partition to bar), ibid., File 121-323; Pettit to Director of Licensing, 5 Aug. 1952, ibid., File 121-350 (gate and floorman, Niagara Hotel); Stanley Hotel, list of notations (electric gate lock), ibid., File 121-362.

34 For examples of the flexible use of 'wandering,' see list of notations for the New Empire Hotel, BCA, GR52, Box 8, File 121-329.

35 List of notations for West Hotel, ibid., Box 9, File 121-366; Haywood to Chairman, 25 March 1949, ibid.; 'Report Made to B.C. Hotels Association RE West Hotel,' 20 July 1949, ibid.; Inspector to Chief Inspector, 24 June 1951, p. 1, ibid., Box 9, File 121-349; McGugan to New Fountain, 21 July 1953, ibid.

36 '?' to Chief Inspector, 2 May 1949, ibid., File 121-358 (Royal); Lythgoe to Chief Inspector, 24 June 1951, ibid., File 121-349 (New Fountain). On women coaxing men, see, for example, Haywood to Chernecki, 10 March 1952, ibid., Box 8, File 121–332 (Grand Union).

37 See, for example, the 1954 blueprints for the Angelus Hotel and Bruce to Acting Director, 2 March 1954, BCA, GR52, Box 7, File 121-311. On telephones, see Pettit to Acting Director, 14 July 1954, ibid., Box 8, File 121-340 (Lotus Hotel).

38 For the Angelus Hotel, see ibid., Box 7, File 121-311, 'Appendix, Annual Report – November 12, 1953' (1st quotation) and 1954 blueprints; for the New Empress Hotel, see Haywood to Chairman, 18 Nov. 1949 (2nd quotation), ibid., Box 9, File 121–348. The New Empress did eventually install somewhat separate entrances, and in early 2000 it was one of two hotels (the other was the Balmoral) that still had not removed the signs over the former separate entrances.

39 'Beer Saloons in Vancouver and Record,' Alcohol Research Education Council, (AREC), BCA, Add. Mss. 17, Vol. 1, File 12.

40 British Columbia, *Revised Statutes of British Columbia*, 1924, c. 146, s. 27(5) (quotation); Murray to Secretary, 22 April 1954, BCA, GR52, Box 9, File 121-368 (interdicted list). On interdiction in general, see British Columbia, *Statutes*, 1921, c. 30, ss. 57–60.

41 Haywood to Chairman, 15 Jan. 1948 (and attached list from West Hotel), BCA, GR52, Box 9, File 121-366.
42 The three investigators' reports are in ibid., File 121-366, as is the inspector's report for 1948 noting that single women could not register.
43 Europe Hotel, 1948 'Inspector's Hotel Report,' ibid., Box 8, File 121-330; New Empire, Brandolini to Director, 10 Oct. 1952, ibid., Box 8, File 121-329; Main, Hanawald to Director, 22 July 1953, ibid., Box 9, File 121-341; Roger Hotel, Bruce to Acting Director, 3 March 1954, ibid., File 121-353.
44 Circular Letter No. 1028, 7 Dec. 1949, Liquor Control and Licensing Branch (LCLB), Victoria, LLCB, Clipping Files.
45 On the significance of treating, see Powers, *Faces along the Bar*, chap. 5.
46 #1 to Chief Inspector, 23 Sept. 1951, BCA, GR52, Box 8, File 121-326 (quotation); Pettit to Supervisor, 28 Sept. 1951, ibid. See also Belmont Hotel, list of notations, 9 April 1953, ibid., Box 7, File 121-315 (sleeping); Haywood to Brockton, 11 March 1950, ibid., File 121-310 (sleeping, Anchor Hotel).
47 Churchill, 'Coming Out in a Cold Climate,' 79; Trower, *Dead Man's Ticket*, 166–8 (quotation).
48 Trower, *Dead Man's Ticket*, 210.
49 Pettigrew and Sikerman, *Forbidden Love*, videocassette. On the importance of working-class bars to the development of lesbian community before the rebirth of the gay liberation movement at the end of the 1960s, see Kennedy and Davis, *Boots of Leather*, and Chamberland, 'Remembering Lesbian Bars.'
50 Pettigrew and Sikerman, *Forbidden Love* (Ruth Christine); Andrea Fatona and Cornelia Wyngaarda, *Hogan's Alley*, videocassette (Leah Curtis). On the Vanport's legal problems, see, for example, *Sun*, 9 Feb., 27 May 1974; *Province*, 7 Jan. 1976. There is no listing for the Vanport in the 1977 telephone directory.
51 On the New Fountain, see in note 35 above the inspector's report dated 24 June 1951 and Chairman to Ely, 17 July 1951, BCA, GR52, Box 9, File 121-349.
52 Churchill, 'Coming Out,' 80–4.
53 Chauncey, *Gay New York*, 2, 348–52; Kennedy and Davis, *Boots of Leather*, 145–6 (quotation on 145).
54 On the purging of the federal civil service, see Robinson and Kimmel, 'The Queer Career.' See also Adams, *The Trouble with Normal*, 23–34; Strong-Boag, 'Home Dreams'; Owram, *Born at the Right Time*, 12–16.
55 Bruce to Acting Director, 21 June 1954, BCA, GR52, Box 10, File 121-381.
56 Chamberland, 'Remembering Lesbian Bars,' 413–'4; Paulson with Simpson, *An Evening*, 13–15. I discuss liquor-related corruption in British Columbia more specifically in chapter 5.

57 Chamberland, 'Remembering Lesbian Bars,' 410. The reference to Ms Ritchie comes from Pettigrew and Sikerman, *Forbidden Love*.

58 I discuss the concept of passing in more detail in chapter 4. On gay codes, including 'gay,' see Chauncey, *Gay New York*, 16–20, 347–9. On the performative qualities of gender, see Butler, *Bodies That Matter*. See also Devor, 'Gender Blending,' iii–iv; Bullough and Bullough, *Cross Dressing*, 238; Feinberg, *Transgender Warriors*, 88–9.

59 On conflating 'lesbian' with 'prostitute,' see Penn, 'The Sexualized Woman,' 359; Chamberland, 'Remembering Lesbian Bars,' 407. See also Adams, 'Youth,' especially 108–15.

60 Pettit to Haywood, 10 July 1952, BCA, GR52, Box 9, File 121-364.

61 Steven Maynard, 'Through a Hole in the Lavatory Wall,' 237; Andrews, 'Sanitary Conveniences,' 21.

62 Valverde, *Diseases of the Will*, 160. On the New Fountain, see the report for June 1951, cited above in note 38.

63 '1' to Chief Inspector, 22 July 1951, BCA, GR52, Box 8, File 121-326 (Dodson). The attorney general was Gordon Wismer. Sharpe to Inspectors, 26 Nov. 1953, RMB, AG, Reel 449.

64 In 1963, for example, the police described the Montreal Cabaret on East Hastings as 'a hangout for queers and appears unsuitable for a [liquor] licence in our opinion.' See 'List of Premises Operating as Cabarets, etc. in Vancouver, B.C.,' [1963] RMB, AG, Reel 619.

65 Freund, 'The Politics of Naming,' 10 (quotation), 78–9.

66 For a good introduction to knowledge, gender, and space, see Spain, *Gendered Spaces*, especially 15–21.

67 Quetel, *History of Syphilis*, 192; Freund, *The Politics of Naming*, 60.

4: Appearance and Performance: Creating and Regulating the Unwanted

1 Pettit to Director, 24 Oct. 1952, BCA, GR52, Box 9, File 121-344; H.Y. to Sir, 20 Oct. 1952, ibid.; Haywood to H.Y., 27 Oct. 1952, ibid. (quotation).

2 Elaine K. Ginsberg, 'Introduction: The Politics of Passing,' in Ginsberg, ed., *Passing and the Fictions of Identity*, 2–4. On the discrediting of the biological assumptions of race, see Anderson, *Vancouver's Chinatown*, especially chap. 1.

3 See above, note 18 to chap. 1.

4 *Province*, 23 Feb. 1940, 11; 'Rogers v. Clarence Hotel et al,' *Western Weekly Reports* 1940 (2): 545–64, quotation at 550.

5 H.Y. to Sir, 20 Oct. 1952, BCA, GR52, Box 9, File 121-344; Buckley to LCB, 9 Feb. 1946, ibid., File 121-359 (St Helens); Lawrence to Wyllie, 9 March 1950, ibid., File 121-357 (Porter letterhead).

6 Fatona and Wyngaarda, *Hogan's Alley*. See also the inspectors' reports for the Stratford and Main hotels.
7 *Province*, 23 Feb. 1940, 11.
8 *Sun*, 23 Aug. 1948, 13.
9 Ward, *White Canada Forever*, 165–6; Buckley to LCB, 9 Feb. 1946, Wyllie to St. Helen's Hotel, 19 Feb. 1946, BCA, GR 52, Box 9, File 121-359; Wyllie to Chief Inspector, 20 Feb. 1946, ibid.; Woods to Wyllie, 26 Feb. 1946, ibid. (quotation).
10 Bruce to Director, 28 Feb. 1953, BCA, GR52, Box 9, File 121-341.
11 Haywood to Gilder, 31 March 1953, ibid., Box 7, File 121-309; Bruce to Director, 27 March 1953, ibid. (1st quotation); Pettit to Director, 24 Oct. 1952, ibid., Box 9, File 121-344 (2nd quotation).
12 '1' to Chief Inspector, 1 Oct. 1950, ibid., Box 9, File 121-364; Haywood to Stratford, 3 Oct. 1950, ibid. In 1948 an agent had described the ladies section of the Stratford as 'full of drunks, mixed couples of white women and male negroes.' See '?' to Chief Inspector, 3 June 1948, ibid. On the Main, see '1' to Chief Inspector, 14 Oct. 1951, ibid., File 121-341; Pettit to Supervisor, 18 Oct. 1951, ibid. David Churchill notes that in the 1950s the Liquor Control Board of Ontario banned mixed-race couples from Toronto's licensed premises. See 'Coming Out in a Cold Climate,' 93.
13 Lemert, *Alcohol*, 309, 319–20; Hawthorn, Belshaw, and Jamieson, *The Indians of British Columbia*, 330, 380. See also Barman, *The West Beyond the West*, 170–2; Barman, 'Taming Aboriginal Sexuality,' 264.
14 Strange and Loo, *Making Good*, 75–8, 121–2. On the long history of anti-Asian hostility in British Columbia, see Ward, *White Canada Forever*, and Roy, *A White Man's Province*.
15 *Fourth AR LCB*, J66 (1st quotation); 'Application for a Beer Licence' (Stratford Hotel), 6 Dec. 1948, BCA, GR48, Box 15, File 2 (2nd quotation). On licensing exclusion of Asians before prohibition, see Ajzenstadt, 'The Medical–Moral Economy of Regulations,' 111–12.
16 Barman, *The West beyond the West*, 379; Bradshaw to Haywood, 9 Jan. 1952, BCA, GR52, Box 8, File 121–340; Haywood to Bradshaw, 10 Jan. 1952, ibid.
17 *Fourth AR LCB* (1925), J66. The LCB required that parlours submit lists of employees' names and where they were eligible to vote.
18 Kennedy to McIntyre, 2 Sept. 1944, BCA, GR770, Box 5, File 2 (126). The hotels that employed Chinese janitors were the Ambassador, American, Balmoral, Carlton, Castle, Commercial, Grandview, Drake (Haddon), Main, Marble Arch, New Fountain, Regent, Royal, St Helen's, and Stanley. The references are all taken from Inspector Files. For the comment of the

inspector at the New Empire, see Bruce to Supervisor, 5 May 1952, BCA, GR52, Box 8, File 121-329.

19 Haywood to Mulligan, 30 March 1948, BCA, GR52, Box 9, File 121–368; Bruce to Director, 17 April 1953, ibid., Box 8, File 121-340. The chief inspector's hand-written comment is on this memo.

20 On the Chinese and gambling, see Anderson, *Vancouver's Chinatown*, 101–4; Ward, *White Canada Forever*, 9–10; Roy, *A White Man's Province*, 16–17; Lai, *Chinatowns*, 195, 229–30; Marquis, 'Vancouver Vice,' 248–51. On the Chinese Democratic Society, see *Province*, 1 Oct. 1951, 17.

21 Pettit to Chief Inspector, 7 Feb. 1951, BCA, GR52, Box 9, File 121-362 (Stanley).

22 Valverde, *Diseases of the Will*, 159.

23 *Revised Statutes of British Columbia* (*RSBC*), 1911, c. 142, s. 64; British Columbia, *Statutes*, 1921, c. 30, s. 11, 35; Vancouver *Sun*, 18 June 1924, 5 (1st quotation); *Province*, 17 Dec. 1924, 1 (Burde).

24 *Fourth AR LCB* (1925), 66 (quotation); British Columbia, *Statutes*, 1924, c. 30, s. 12.

25 *Sixth AR LCB* (1927), 6. Prosecutions for supplying liquor to a minor also included buying liquor for a minor at a government liquor store.

26 *Province*, 16 Nov. 1932, 1.

27 Ibid.

28 *Colonist*, 18 Nov. 1932, 3. On the signification of 'youth' as male and a social problem, see Adams, *The Trouble with Normal*, 40.

29 *Province*, 17 Dec., 1924, 1; Powers, *Faces along the Bar*, 36 (quotation)–41; Kimmel, *Manhood in America*, 124–5.

30 [Unnamed] to Chief Inspector, 19 Dec. 1947, BCA, GR52, Box 8, File 121-320; Pettit to Director, 17 July 1953, ibid, Box 9, File 121-341 (Main). See also Pettit to Chief Inspector, 30 May 1950, ibid, Box 8, File 121-318.

31 *Province*, 25 May 1950, 17; Kahn to Wyllie, 30 Jan. 1943, BCA, GR770, Box 5, File 199B.

32 British Columbia, *Statutes*, 1947, c. 53, ss. 12, 14.

33 List of notations, Burrard Hotel, BCA, GR52, Box 8, File 121-317; Penal to Wismer, 29 January 1951, RMB, AG, Reel 371, File L217-2; General Secretary-Treasurer to Wismer, 9 Feb. 1951, ibid. See also Victoria Labour Council to Bonner, June 1957, RMB, AG, Reel 449.

34 British Columbia, *Statutes*, 1953, c. 166, ss. 59, 61, 101; Morrison to Vancouver and District Labour Council, 17 Oct. 1966, CVA, HRCEBU, Vol. 1, File 5.

35 Leland, *Firewater Myths*, 1.

36 Mancall, *Deadly Medicine*, 6 (1st quotation), 28 (2nd quotation). See also

Smart and Ogborne, *Northern Spirits*, 106; Fisher, 'Alcoholism and Race.' Many years ago Judge F.W. Howay argued that 'the Indian of the Northwest Coast had no inborn desire for or knowledge of intoxicating liquor, and his first reaction to it was one of disgust.' See Howay, 'Introduction,' 46. More recently, Jan Noel has argued, 'We still do not know very much about the ways in which alcohol transformed native cultures. The evidence of traders, missionaries, and settlers on the deleterious effects of drink, at least in the early nineteenth century, tends to be overwhelming.' She adds that Natives and sailors had similar drinking patterns and that 'Indians were not the only ones, though, who fell prey to fiery fluids.' See Noel, *Canada Dry*, 183 (1st quotation), 187–8 (2nd quotation).

37 Tobias, 'Protection, Civilization, Assimilation,' 41, 44; Simons, 'Liquor Control.'

38 Megan Schlase, 'Liquor,' 26; Valverde, *Diseases of the Will*, 165–6.

39 'B.C. Laws pertaining to liquor control,' RMB, AG, Reel 372; British Columbia, *Statutes*, 1921, c. 30, s. 11, 36, 57–60. On legislation on drunkards, see British Columbia, *Revised Statutes of British Columbia*, 1897, c. 66 and c. 124, ss. 8–10; *Vancouver Sun*, 14 Oct. 1959, 21 (Walkem quotation).

40 Hose, *Prohibition or Control?*, 64; *Victoria Times*, 3 Aug. 1926 (quotation).

41 'Tenth Annual convention,' p. 2 (1st quotation), 3 (2nd quotation), BCA, Add. Mss. 17, AREC, Vol. 29, File 'Minutes of Meetings 1925–1926'; McIntyre to Kennedy, 13 July 1940, BCA, GR770, Box 2, File 27 (old File 126), (3rd quotation).

42 'Regulations Governing all Employees in Beer Parlours Operated by Company,' BCA, GR52, Box 9, File 121–368 (1st quotation); Wyllie to Dominion Hotel, 4 July 1939, ibid., Box 8, File 121-327 (2nd quotation); Kennedy to McIntyre, 3 Dec. 1942, GR770, Box 2, File 126-1 (3rd quotation).

43 Frideres, *Native People in Canada*, 6–9 (1st quotation); Wyllie to Peterson, 21 Sept. 1948, BCA, GR52, Box 9, File 121-357 (2nd and 3rd quotations).

44 Statement of NE, 30 Nov. 1949, BCA, GR52, Box 9, File 121-353 (1st quotation); Branca to Haywood, 5 Dec. 1949, ibid. (2nd quotation); Haywood to Secretary, 8 Dec. 1949, ibid. (3rd quotation).

45 #1 to Chief Inspector, 1 Nov. 1950, ibid., Box 8, File 121-326; Haywood to Dodson, 3 Nov. 1950, ibid. A similar lack of official interest was shown at the Stanley in July 1951; see #1 to Chief Inspector, 27 July 1951, ibid., Box 9, File 121-362, and Haywood to Secretary, 30 July 1951, ibid.

46 On city police enforcement, see Wyllie to Regent, 29 May 1946, ibid., Box 9, File 121-357, and Campbell to Secretary, 24 Sept. 1947, ibid., File 121-362.

47 See Kimberly to Chief Inspector, 19 March 1948, ibid., Box 8, File 121-335;

Kimberly to Chief Inspector, 23 March 1948, ibid.; Chief Inspector to Secretary, 30 March 1948, ibid. (quotation).

48 Kimberly to Chief Inspector, 30 April 1949, ibid., Box 9, File 121-345; Agent to Chief Inspector, 2 May 1949, ibid.; Chief Inspector to Secretary, 6 May 1949, ibid. (quotation); British Columbia, *Statutes*, 1947, c. 53, s. 16.

49 Haywood to Secretary, 8 Dec. 1949, BCA, GR52, Box 9, File 121-353.

50 Miller, *Skyscrapers Hide the Heavens*, 220–2; Moran, *Stoney Creek Woman*, 106–7; Hawthorn, Belshaw, and Jamieson, *Indians of British Columbia*, 331–2.

51 *Province*, 13 Dec. 1951, 17.

52 Bruce to Director of Licensing, 18 April 1953, BCA, GR52, Box 9, File 121-345 (1st quotation); Haywood to Melbourne Hotel, 22 April 1953, ibid. (2nd quotation); Brandolini to Haywood, 14 May 1953, ibid. (3rd quotation). For a similar example from the Stanley, see Bruce to Director, 18 April 1953, ibid., File 121-362.

53 *Province*, 24 Dec. 1951, 1; Hawthorn, Belshaw and Jamieson, *Indians of British Columbia*, 332 (RCMP quotation), 382.

54 Lythgoe to Supervisor, 21 Feb. 1952, BCA, GR52, Box 10, File 121-386.

55 Haywood to Kelway, 26 February 1952, ibid. Racial segregation had long existed in South Africa, but it was extended with the election of the National party in 1948. See, for example, Regehr, *Perceptions of Apartheid*, 26–7.

56 Segregated facilities did exist. Historian Barry Broadfoot remembered drinking in the 1950s in one of Squamish's beer parlours, which had a separate area, bordered by a white line, for Native drinkers. Native people who did not feel comfortable within those limits would bring condoms and have them filled beer. With these unusual growlers they would leave and drink elsewhere. Personal communication, 4 March 1997.

Based on the stories of 75 people, Brian Maracle has written a fascinating account of the experiences of Aboriginal people with alcohol and other drugs. One provides a combined account of passing and an explicit ban on Native people in BC beer parlours. In the early 1970s, Kathy, a Cree woman, got a job in a Kamloops beer parlour. A bartender ordered her not to serve some Native people, as the facility banned all Natives. She asked him if it allowed Indians to work there. He laughed and said, 'Oh, fuck no.' Her response: 'So I threw my tray on him and climbed over the bar and tried to kill him.' See Maracle, *Crazywater*, 79–80 (quotations).

57 Lythgoe to Supervisor, 14 Sept. 1951, BCA, GR52, Box 10, File 121-386; Haywood to Kelway, 25 Sept. 1951, ibid. (quotations); Kelway to Haywood, 31 Oct. 1951, ibid.

58 Report of Cpl W. West, 14 April 1952, ibid., Kelway to Haywood, 23 June 1952 (1st quotation), ibid.; Kelway to Haywood, 3 July 1952 (2nd quotation), ibid.

59 Lythgoe to Director, 7–13 Aug. 1952, ibid.

60 Lythgoe to Director, 11 Nov. 1952, ibid. (1st quotation); Lythgoe to Director, 28 Dec. 1953, ibid.; Lythgoe to Acting Director, 15 May 1954, ibid. (2nd quotation).

61 *Province*, 14 May 1954, 2.

62 Young to Haywood, 29 Feb. 1952, BCA, GR52, Box 10, File 121-398 (RCMP and Paull); Lythgoe to Director, Nov. 1953, ibid., Box 7, File 121-293.

63 *Vancouver Herald*, 2 March 1953, 16; Moran, *Stoney Creek Woman*, 107; Hawthorn, Belshaw, and Jamieson, *Indians of British Columbia*, 381.

64 Lemert, *Alcohol*, 356 (1st quotation); 346 (2nd quotation); Hawthorn, Belshaw, and Jamieson, *Indians of British Columbia*, 332–3 (3rd quotation), 382 (4th quotation). In 1954 the government of Manitoba appointed a commission to study liquor issues in the province. Its 1955 report recommended, 'on a two year trial basis,' that 'Indians in Manitoba be legally permitted to enter licensed premises and to purchase and consume liquor therein and that they be allowed to purchase liquor for off-premise consumption in a residence other than where prohibited by federal law.' Its assumption was that liquor equality would promote – in the words of an unnamed 'prominent official of the Indian Health Services in Ottawa' – the 'complete assimilation of the Indian' See Manitoba, *Report of the Liquor Enquiry Commission. Part 2*, 615, 614.

65 Lemert, *Alcohol*, 321–2; Hawthorn, Belshaw, and Jamieson, *Indians*, 380–1; Moran, *Stoney Creek Woman*, 108–9; *Province*, 14 May 1954, 2 (Paull), 4 July 1962, 1; Barman, *The West beyond the West*, 379; Valverde, *Diseases of the Will*, 167.

5: Reconfiguring Decency in the 1950s: The Politics of Regulation

1 *Province*, 12 July 1949, 2. Monks had been refused service in a beer pralour in London, Ontario.

2 I discussed these issues in more detail in *Demon Rum or Easy Money*, 82, 86–90, 92–3, 191.

3 Valverde, *Disease of the Will*, 96–7 (quotation on 96).

4 *Province*, 6 Aug. 1945, 20 (Sexton), 21 July 1945, 4 (dismal), 21 Nov. 1946, 4 (sterilized), 22 March 1946, 9 (Gargrave); *Daily Colonist*, 4 March 1947 (Hodges).

5 Kennedy to Wismer, 17 Feb. 1947, RMB, AG, Reel 371; Campbell, *Demon Rum*, 93; *Province*, 15 July 1949, 36 (poll).

6 Canadian Restaurant Association to Wismer, 14 Feb. 1947, RMB, AG, Reel 371; *Province*, 29 Feb. 1952, 38 (quotation).

7 On cabarets in general, see Jeff Bateman, 'Big Bands,' in Chuck Davis, ed., *The Greater Vancouver Book: An Urban Encyclopaedia*, 698, and Leiren-Young, 'History of Entertainment,' in ibid., 719–22. See also *Province*, 4 Jan. 1949, 9, 29 May 1950, 1–2; *Colonist*, 5 Jan. 1949; 'There's Always Somebody Who Wants the Liquor Law Changed!' B.C. Cabaret Owners pamphlet, 1949, RMB, AG, Reel 371.

8 British Columbia, *Statutes*, 1947, c. 53, s. 9; Haywood to the Chairman, 21 June 1948, RMB, AG, Reel 619; *Sun*, 18 June 1948, 1. On Washington state, see Clark, *The Dry Years*, 243, 248–50.

9 *Province*, 23 Jan. 1952, 1; Adams, 'A Study,' 134.

10 Small to Wismer, 15 March 1950, RMB, AG, Reel 372 (1st quotation); 'BCTL Executive Meeting,' 10 March 1952, BCA, AREC, Add. Mss. 17, Vol. 2, File 20 (2nd quotation).

11 'Report for 1952,' BCA, Add. Mss. 17, Vol. 20, File, '1952'; BCTL Executive Meeting,' 10 March 1952, ibid., Vol. 2, File 20 (1st quotation); Cowley to Linton, n.d., ibid., Vol. 3, File 25 (2nd quotation). The Temperance League was the product of an earlier name change. After the United States abandoned prohibition in 1933, the B.C. Prohibition Association renamed itself the B.C. Temperance League.

12 *Sun*, 22 April 1940, 18; *Province*, 5 May 1952, 5 (1st quotation), 6 May 1952, 3 (2nd quotation); Clark, *The Dry Years*, 248; *Sun*, 10 June 1952, 4 (editorial). On post-war modernism and consumerism, see Owram, *Born at the Right Time*, 75–9, and Parr, 'Shopping for a Good Stove,' especially 82–90.

13 'Statement of Result of Liquor Plebiscite – June 12, 1952,' RMB, AG, Reel 373; 'The Canadian Temperance Federation Minutes of the Executive Meeting,' 24 June 1952, BCA, Add. Mss. 17, Vol. 3, File 26 (quotation).

14 On temperance groups appearing before the commission, see Alcohol Research Council to Commission, 19 Nov. 1952, BCA, Add. Mss. 17, Vol. 20, File '1952'; *Province*, 9 Oct. 1952, 23; *Sun*, 20 Nov. 1952, 2.

15 Mills to Wismer, 8 March 1950, RMB, AG, Reel 371; *Province*, 9 June 1952, 3, 16 Oct. 1952, 21.

16 Local 676 Executive Meeting, 9 Nov. 1952, UBC, SC, HRCEBU, Box 6, Minute Book, 25 May 1952–14 Feb. 1955 (quotations). See also Local Joint Executive Minutes, 7 Jan. 1959, ibid., Box 7, LJEB (Local Joint Executive Board), Minute Book, 8 Jan. 1958–2 Jan. 1974.

17 *Colonist*, 15 Jan. 1947 (1st quotation); *Province*, 22 Nov. 1952; BCHA to Retail Clerks Union, 21 Aug. 1953, RMB, AG, Reel 449; *Province*, 20 Aug. 1953, 33 (2nd quotation).

18 *Province*, 20 Nov. 1952, 13.

19 Ibid., 19 Nov. 1952, 21, 3 Dec. 1952, 1. The four hotels toured were the Stanley and the Manitoba, on Cordova Street, and the Haddon (later Drake) and the Princeton, on Powell Street.

20 British Columbia, *Report of the Liquor Inquiry Commission 1952*, 11; *Province*, 3 Dec. 1952, 1 (quotation).

21 British Columbia, *Liquor Inquiry Commission*, 14–16.

22 Ibid., 7.

23 While we differ somewhat in our conclusions, my reading of corruption was inspired by Loo and Strange, 'The Traveling Show Menace,' 645–9.

24 Victoria *Times*, 2 April 1951, 4; *Sun*, 18 June 1948, 1 (quotations in previous paragraph). I cite the disgruntled operator's account above in note 18 to chapter 1. On the Quadra Club, see *Sun*, 16 Jan. 1986, A3.

25 *Sun*, 18 June 1948, 1. On the links between political parties and newspapers, see Rutherford, *A Victorian Authority*. For a lively discussion of the competitive world of Vancouver's three daily papers in the 1950s, see Macdonald and O'Keefe, *The Mulligan Affair*, 42–55.

26 British Columbia, *Liquor Inquiry Commission*, 8, 16, 18, 26–7.

27 Ibid., 8–9.

28 Ibid., 17, 23 (quotation).

29 Beddome to Bonner, 22 January 1953, RMB, AG, Reel 448; Mangles to Premier, 23 January 1953, ibid.; *Province*, 30 Jan. 1953, 1.

30 British Columbia Bill 21, 'Explanatory Notes,' 1; *33rd AR LCB* (1954), 38.

31 *33rd AR LCB* (1954), 7, 38; Galloway to Bonner, 11 Oct. 1953, RMB, AG, Reel 449; Special membership meeting, 11 Oct. 1953, UBC, SC, HRCEBU, Box 6, Minute Book, May 1952–Feb. 1955; *Province*, 23 Nov. 1954, 3 (Johnson).

32 *33rd AR LCB* (1954), 5; Bonner to Bracken, 21 June 1954, RMB, AG, Reel 449; *Province*, 20 Oct. 1954, 14, 21 Dec. 1954, 34.

33 Victoria *Times*, 20 Oct. 1953, 1; *Province*, 10 April 1954, 1–2; *News-Herald*, 21 Jan. 1954, 1, 13 March 1954; *Province*, 2 June 1954, 6.

34 *Sun*, 28 June 1954, 32.

35 *News-Herald*, 21 Jan. 1954, 1; Valverde, *Diseases of the Will*, 157.

36 Owram, *Born at the Right Time*, 90 (quotation), 19–23.The regulations were published in *33rd AR LCB* (1954), Q36–40.

37 *Province*, 14 Oct. 1953, p. 1–2; Lanza, *The Cocktail*, 77. On cocktails, see also Edmunds, *The Silver Bullet*, 66–70; Gray, *Bacchanalia Revisited*, 54–7.

38 *Province*, 22 Feb. 1947, 9 (1st quotation); 14 Sept. 1953, 6 (2nd quotation),

1 Oct. 1953, 6, 3 Oct. 1953, 45 (3rd quotation). See also *Sun*, 20 Nov. 1952, 2, for the comments of a hotel representative grown tired of references to British pubs.

39 James H. Gray has described the looser attitudes towards alcohol, gender, and leisure after the war. See *Bacchanalia Revisited*, 93–8. As of December 1963, parlours were allowed to remove their partitions. See *Sun*, 3 Dec. 1963, 1.

40 *33rd AR LCB* (1954), 39; Victoria *Times*, 2 July 1954, 15. A former bartender at the Sylvia informed me of the lounge's policy.

41 Kimmel, *Manhood in America*, 124, 234–8; May, *Homeward Bound*, 87–8; Owram, *Born at the Right Time*, 14–16; Gray, *Bacchanalia Revisited*, 56; Valverde, *Diseases of the Will*, 106–8.

42 Lanza, *The Cocktail*, 128–30; Kimmel, *Manhood in America*, 255 (quotation).

43 *Province* 14 Sept. 1953, 6; 1 Oct. 1953, 6.

Conclusion: Managing the Marginal

1 Sangster, 'Incarcerating "Bad Girls,"' 242. See also, Valverde, comp., *Radically Rethinking Regulation*. On the net metaphor, see Strange and Loo, *Making Good*, 5–6; Loo, 'Dan Cramner's Potlatch,' 165; Foucault, *Power/Knowledge*, 39, 98.

2 Strange and Loo, *Making Good*, 149.

3 Ibid., 149–51.

4 This paragraph takes its lead from the venerable and durable overview by Leo Panitch. See his 'The Role and Nature of the Canadian State,' in Panitch, ed., *The Canadian State*, 3–27, quotation at 4. For a more recent review of state literature, see Baehre, 'The State in Canadian History.'

5 Corrigan and Sayer, *The Great Arch*, 197; Mark Leier, *Red Flags & Red Tape*, 36–8, quotations at 37.

6 On coercion and consent, see Hay, *Re-Stating*, 25–7.

7 Anderson, *Vancouver's Chinatown*, 20, 24; Said, *Orientalism*.

8 Sheriff, 'State Theory,' 672; Ashforth, 'Reckoning Schemes of Legitimation,' 4, 12. See also Burton and Carlen, *Official Discourse*, 7–14.

9 Hay, *Re-Stating*, 5–8 (quotation); Corrigan and Sayer, *The Great Arch*, 180. See also Lears, 'The Concept of Cultural Hegemony,' 588; Abrams, 'Notes,' 82.

References

Archival Collections

B.C. Provincial Secretary and Government Services, Records Management Branch (RMB)

Attorney General Correspondence, 1938–1965 (transferred to the British Columbia Archives, below, as GR1723–6)

British Columbia Archives (BCA)

Add. Mss. 17   Alcohol Research and Education Council (AREC), (B.C. Temperance League)
GR48   B.C. Liquor Control Board (LCB), Beer Licence Files
GR52   B.C. Liquor Control Board, Inspector Files
GR62   B.C. Liquor Control Board, Scrapbooks
GR770   B.C. Liquor Control Board, General Collection
GR1323   B.C. Attorney General Correspondence, 1902–37
GR1723   Attorney General Correspondence (c. 1938–52)
GR1724   Attorney General Correspondence (c. 1952–9)
GR1725   Attorney General Correspondence (c. 1959–65)
GR1726   Attorney General Correspondence (c. 1959–72)

For GR1723–6, access, even to the full finding aids, is now quite restricted under the Freedom of Information and Protection of Privacy Act.

British Columbia Liquor Control and Licensing Branch (LCLB), Victoria

B.C. Liquor Control Board, Minutes of Meetings
LCLB, Clippings File

University of British Columbia (UBC), Special Collections and Archives Division (SC)

Angus MacInnis Memorial Collection
Hotel, Restaurant and Culinary Employees and Bartenders Union, Local 40 (HRCEBU – UBC)
International Union of Mine, Mill and Smelter Workers (Canada)
Vancouver Council of Women
Vancouver and District Labour Council (V&DLC – UBC)

City of Vancouver Archives (CVA)

Hotel, Restaurant and Culinary Employees and Bartenders Union, Local 40 (HRCEBU – CVA)
Pacific Press News Clippings (Series I and II)
Vancouver Council of Women

Published Government Material

Annual Report of the Liquor Control Board of the Province of British Columbia (no. AR LCB), Victoria: various years.
British Columbia. *Report of the Liquor Inquiry Commission 1952*. Victoria: Queen's Printer, 1953.
British Columbia. *Revised Statutes of British Columbia (RSBC)*. 1897. c. 66 ('Habitual Drunkards Act').
– *RSBC*. 1897. c. 124 ('Liquor Traffic Regulation Act').
– *RSBC*. 1911. c. 142 ('Liquor Licence Act').
– *Statutes*. 1919. c. 88 ('Venereal Diseases Suppression Act').
– *Statutes*. 1921. c. 30 ('Government Liquor Act').
– *RSBC*. 1924. c. 146. ('Government Liquor Act').
– *Statutes*. 1924. c. 30 (Government Liquor Act Amendment Act, 1924')
– *Statutes*. 1947. c. 53 ('Government Liquor Act Amendment Act, 1947').
– *Statutes*. 1947. c. 95 ('Venereal Diseases Suppression Act').
– *Statutes*. 1953. c. 166 (Government Liquor Act).
– *Revised Statutes*. 1960. c. 14 ('Government Liquor Act, 1953').
Manitoba. *Report of the Liquor Enquiry Commission*. Winnipeg, 1955.

Newspapers (titles vary slightly)

British Columbia Federationist (Vancouver).
Vancouver *News-Herald*.

Vancouver *Province*.
Vancouver *Sun*.
Victoria *Colonist*.
Victoria *Times*.

Theses and Dissertations

Adams, Audrey Marilyn. 'A Study of the Use of Plebiscites and Referendums by the Province of British Columbia.' MA thesis, University of British Columbia, 1958.

Ajzenstadt, Mimi. 'The Medical–Moral Economy of Regulations: Alcohol Legislation in B.C., 1871–1925.' PhD dissertation, Simon Fraser University, 1992.

Christie, Howard Angus. 'The Function of the Tavern in Toronto 1834–1875 with Special Reference to Sport.' MPE thesis, University of Windsor, 1973.

Churchill, David S. 'Coming Out in a Cold Climate: A History of Gay Men in Toronto during the 1950s.' MA Thesis, University of Toronto, 1993.

Devor, Holly. 'Gender Blending: When Two Is Not Enough.' MA thesis, Simon Fraser University, 1985.

Freund, Michaela. 'The Politics of Naming: Constructing Prostitutes and Regulating Women in Vancouver, 1934–1945.' MA thesis, Simon Fraser University, 1995.

Hiebert, Albert John. 'Prohibition in British Columbia.' MA thesis, Simon Fraser University, 1969.

Padmavathy, V. 'The English Barmaid, 1874–1914: A Case Study of Unskilled and Non-unionized Women Workers.' PhD dissertation, Miami University, Ohio, 1989.

Rose, Ramona Marie '"Keepers of Morale": The Vancouver Council of Women, 1939–1945.' MA thesis, University of British Columbia, 1990.

Simons, Nicholas J.S. 'Liquor Control and the Native Peoples of Western Canada.' MA thesis, Simon Fraser University, 1992.

Weiss, Gillian. '"As Women and as Citizens": Clubwomen in Vancouver, 1910–1928.' PhD dissertation, University of British Columbia, 1983.

Articles, Books, and Videocassettes

Abrams, Philip. 'Notes on the Difficulty of Studying the State (1977).' *Journal of Historical Sociology* 1 (March 1988): 58–89.

Adams, Mary Louise. 'In Sickness and in Health: State Formation, Moral

Regulation, and Early VD Initiatives in Ontario.' *Journal of Canadian Studies* 28 (winter 1993–4): 117–30.

– '"Almost anything can happen": A Search for Sexual Discourse in the Urban Spaces of 1940s Toronto.' *Canadian Journal of Sociology* 19 (1994): 217–232.

– 'Youth, Corruptibility, and English-Canadian Postwar Campaigns against Indecency, 1948–1955.' *Journal of the History of Sexuality* 6 (1995): 89–117.

– *The Trouble with Normal: Post-war Youth and the Making of Heterosexuality.* Toronto: University of Toronto Press, 1997.

Ahlstrom, Salme. 'Cultural Differences in Women's Drinking.' *Contemporary Drug Problems* 22 (fall 1995): 393–414.

Anderson, Kay. J. *Vancouver's Chinatown: Racial Discourse in Canada, 1875–1980.* Montreal: McGill-Queen's University Press, 1991.

Andrews, Margaret W. 'Sanitary Conveniences and the Retreat of the Frontier: Vancouver, 1886–1926.' *BC Studies* 87 (autumn 1990): 3–22.

Ashforth, Adam. 'Reckoning Schemes of Legitimation: On Commissions of Inquiry as Power/Knowledge Forms.' *Journal of Historical Sociology* 3 (1990): 1–22.

Bacchi, Carol. 'Race Regeneration and Social Purity: A Study of the Social Attitudes of Canada's English-Speaking Suffragists.' In R. Douglas Francis and Donald B. Smith, eds., *Readings in Canadian History: Post-Confederation*, 2nd ed., 308–21. Toronto: Holt, 1986. Originally published in *Histoire sociale/Social History* 11 (Nov. 1978): 460–74.

Baehre, Rainer. 'The State in Canadian History.' *Acadiensis* 24 (autumn 1994): 119–33.

Bailey, Peter. 'Parasexuality and Glamour: The Victorian Barmaid as Cultural Prototype.' *Gender and History* 2 (summer 1990): 148–72.

Barman, Jean. *The West beyond the West: A History of British Columbia.* Rev. ed. Toronto: University of Toronto Press, 1996.

– 'Taming Aboriginal Sexuality: Gender, Power, and Race in British Columbia, 1850–1900.' *BC Studies* 115–16 (autumn–winter 1997–8): 237–66.

Baron, Ava. 'On Looking at Men: Masculinity and the Making of a Gendered Working-Class History.' In Ann-Louise Shapiro, ed., *Feminists Revision History*, 146–71. New Brunswick, NJ: Rutgers University Press, 1994.

Barrows, Susanna, and Robin Room, eds. *Drinking: Behavior and Belief in Modern History.* Berkeley: University of California Press, 1991.

Bennett, Judith M. 'The Village Ale-Wife: Women and Brewing in Fourteenth Century England.' In B. Hanawalt, ed., *Women and Work in Preindustrial Europe*, 20–36. Bloomington: University of Indiana Press, 1986.

– *Ale, Beer and Brewsters in England: Women's Work in a Changing World, 1300–1600.* New York: Oxford University Press, 1996.

Bliss, Michael '"Pure Books on Avoided Subjects": Pre-Freudian Sexual Ideas in Canada.' Canadian Historical Association, *Historical Papers* (1970): 89–108.

Blocker, Jack S., and Cheryl Krasnick Warsh, eds. *The Changing Face of Drink: Substance, Imagery, and Behaviour*. Ottawa: Les Publications Histoire social/Social History, 1997.

Blomley, Nicholas K. 'Text and Context: Rethinking the Law-Space Nexus.' *Progress in Human Geography* 13 (1989): 512–34.

Brennan, Thomas. *Public Drinking and Popular Culture in Eighteenth-Century Paris*. Princeton, NJ: Princeton University Press, 1988.

Buckley, Suzann, and Janice McGinnis. 'Venereal Disease and Public Health Reform in Canada.' *Canadian Historical Review* 63 (Sept. 1982): 337–54.

Bullough, Vern L., and Bonnie Bullough. *Cross Dressing, Sex, and Gender*. Philadelphia: University of Pennsylvania Press, 1993.

Burchell, Graham, Colin Gordon, and Peter Miller, eds. *The Foucault Effect: Studies in Governmentality*. London: Harvester Wheatsheaf, 1991.

Burton, Frank, and Pat Carlen. *Official Discourse: On Discourse Analysis, Government Publications, Ideology and the State*. London: Routledge, 1979.

Butler, Judith. *Gender Trouble: Feminism and the Subversion of Identity*. New York: Routledge, 1990.

– *Bodies That Matter: On the Discursive Limits of 'Sex.'* New York: Routledge, 1993.

Campbell, Robert A. 'Liquor and Liberals: Patronage and Government Control in British Columbia, 1920–1928.' *BC Studies* 77 (spring 1988): 30–53.

– *Demon Rum or Easy Money: Government Control of Liquor in British Columbia from Prohibition to Privatization*. Ottawa: Carleton University Press, 1991.

– '"Profit was just a circumstance": The Evolution of Government Liquor Control in British Columbia, 1920–1988.' In Cheryl Krasnick Warsh, ed., *Drink in Canada: Historical Essays*, 172–92. Montreal: McGill-Queen's University Press, 1993.

– 'Ladies and Escorts: Gender Segregation and Public Policy in British Columbia Beer Parlours, 1925–1945.' *BC Studies* 105–6 (spring–summer 1995): 119–38.

– 'Managing the Marginal: Regulating and Negotiating Decency in Vancouver's Beer Parlours, 1925–1954.' *Labour/LeTravail* 44 (fall 1999), 109–27.

Canning, Kathleen. *Languages of Labor and Gender: Female Factory Work in Germany, 1850–1914*. Ithaca, NY: Cornell University Press, 1996.

Cassel, Jay. *The Secret Plague: Venereal Disease in Canada, 1838–1939*. Toronto: University of Toronto Press, 1987.

Chamberland, Line. 'Remembering Lesbian Bars: Montreal, 1955–1975.' In

Veronica Strong-Boag and Anita Clair Fellman, eds., *Rethinking Canada: The Promise of Women's History*, 3rd ed., 402–23. Don Mills, Ont.: Oxford University Press, 1997.

Chauncey, George. *Gay New York: Gender, Urban Culture, and the Making of the Gay Male World*. New York: Basic Books, 1994.

Clark, Norman H. *The Dry Years: Prohibition and Social Change in Washington*. Rev. ed. Seattle: University of Washington Press, 1988.

Clark, Peter. *The English Alehouse: A Social History 1200–1830*. London: Longman, 1983.

Cobble, Dorothy Sue. *Dishing It Out: Waitresses and Their Unions in the Twentieth Century*. Urbana, Ill.: University of Illinois Press, 1991.

Cohen, Stanley. 'The Critical Discourse on "Social Control": Notes on the Concept as a Hammer.' *International Journal of the Sociology of Law* 17 (1989): 347–57.

Conroy, David W. *In Public Houses: Drink and the Revolution of Authority in Colonial Massachusetts*. Chapel Hill: University of North Carolina Press, 1995.

Cook, Sharon Anne. *'Through Sunshine and Shadow': The Woman's Christian Temperance Union, Evangelicalism, and Reform in Ontario, 1874–1930*. Montreal: McGill-Queen's University Press, 1995.

Corrigan, Philip, and Derek Sayer. *The Great Arch: English State Formation as Cultural Revolution*. Oxford: Basil Blackwell, 1985.

Cutler, R.E., and Thomas Storm. 'Observational Study of Alcohol Consumption in Natural Settings: The Vancouver Beer Parlor.' *Journal of Studies on Alcohol* 36 (1975): 1173–83.

Davis, Chuck, ed. *The Greater Vancouver Book: An Urban Encyclopaedia*. Surrey, BC: Linkman Press, 1997.

Dean, Mitchell '"A social structure of many souls": Moral Regulation, Government, and Self-formation.' *Canadian Journal of Sociology* 19 (1994): 145–68.

DeLottinville, Peter. 'Joe Beef of Montreal: Working Class Culture and the Tavern, 1869–1889.' *Labour/Le Travailleur* 8 and 9 (autumn and spring 1981–2): 9–40.

Douglas, Mary, ed. *Constructive Drinking: Perspectives on Drink from Anthropology*. Cambridge: Cambridge University Press, 1987.

Duis, Perry R. *The Saloon: Public Drinking in Chicago and Boston, 1880–1920*. Chicago: University of Chicago Press, 1983.

Dunk, Thomas. *It's a Working-Man's Town: Male Working-Class Culture in Northwestern Ontario*. Montreal: McGill-Queen's University Press, 1991.

Edmunds, Lowell. *The Silver Bullet: The Martini in American Civilization*. Westport, Conn.: Greenwood Press, 1981.

Fatona, Andrea, and Wyngaarda, Cornelia, prods. and dirs. *Hogan's Alley*. Videocassette. 33 minutes.Vancouver: Video Out, 1993.

Feinberg, Leslie. *Transgender Warriors: Making History from Joan of Arc to Rupaul*. Boston: Beacon Press, 1996.

Fingard, Judith. '"A Great Big Rum Shop": The Drink Trade in Victorian Halifax.' In J. Morrison and J. Moreira, eds., *Tempered By Rum: Rum in the History of the Maritime Provinces*, 89–102. Porters Lake, NS: Pottersfield Press, 1988.

– *The Dark Side of Victorian Halifax*. Porters Lake, NS: Pottersfield Press, 1989.

Fisher, A.D. 'Alcoholism and Race: The Misapplication of Both Concepts to North American Indians.' *Canadian Review of Sociology and Anthropology* 24 (1987): 81–98.

Foucault, Michel. *The History of Sexuality*. Vol. 1, *An Introduction*. Trans. Robert Hurley. London: Allen Lane, 1978; reprint, New York: Vintage Books, 1990.

– *Power/Knowledge: Selected Interviews and Other Writings, 1972–1977*. Ed. Colin Gordon. New York: Pantheon Books, 1980.

– 'Governmentality.' In Burchell, Gordon, and Miller, eds., *The Foucault Effect*, 87–104.

Frader, Laura L. 'Dissent over Discourse: Labor History, Gender, and the Linguistic Turn.' *History and Theory* 34 (1995): 213–30.

Frideres, James S. *Native People in Canada: Contemporary Conflicts*. Scarborough, Ont.: Prentice Hall, 1983.

Gefou-Madianou, Dimitra. 'Introduction: Alcohol, Commensality, Identity Transformations and Transcendence.' In Dimitra Gefou-Madianou, ed., *Alcohol, Gender and Culture*, 1–34. London: Routledge, 1992.

Ginsberg, Elaine K. 'Introduction: The Politics of Passing.' In Elaine K. Ginsberg, ed., *Passing and the Fictions of Identity*, 1–18. Durham, NC: Duke University Press, 1996.

Gray, James, H. *Booze: The Impact of Whisky on the Prairie West*. Toronto: Macmillan, 1972.

– *The Roar of the Twenties*. Toronto: Macmillan, 1975.

– *Bacchanalia Revisited: Western Canada's Boozy Skid to Social Disaster*. Saskatoon: Western Producer Prairie Books, 1982.

Griffiths, N.E.S. *The Splendid Vision: Centennial History of the National Council of Women of Canada, 1893–1993*. Ottawa: Carleton University Press, 1993.

Groth, Paul. *Living Downtown: The History of Residential Hotels in the United States*. Berkeley: University of California Press, 1994.

Guillet, Edwin Clarence. *Pioneer Inns and Taverns*, combined ed. 2 vols. Toronto: Ontario Publishing Co., 1964.

Gutzke, David. 'Gentrifying the British Public House, 1896–1914.' *International Labor and Working-Class History* 45 (spring 1994): 29–43.

– 'Gender, Class, and Public Drinking in Britain during the First World War.'
  Histoire sociale/Social History 27 (Nov. 1994): 367–91. Reprinted in Blocker
  and Warsh, eds., *The Changing Face of Drink*, 291–320.

Haine, W. Scott. *The World of the Parisian Cafe: Sociability among the French
  Working Class*. Baltimore, Md.: Johns Hopkins University Press, 1996.

Hawthorn, Harry B., C.S. Belshaw, and S.M. Jamieson. *The Indians of British
  Columbia: A Study of Contemporary Social Adjustment*. Toronto: University of
  Toronto Press, 1958.

Hay, Colin. *Re-Stating Social and Political Change*. Buckingham: Open University Press, 1996.

Hey, Valerie. *Patriarchy and Pub Culture*. London: Tavistock, 1986.

Hoare, Quintin, and Geoffrey Nowell Smith, eds. and trans. *Selections from the
  Prison Notebooks of Antonio Gramsci*. New York: International Publishers,
  1971.

Hose, Reginald. *Prohibition or Control? Canada's Experience with the Liquor
  Problem, 1921– 1927*. New York: Longmans, Green and Co., 1928

Howay, F.W. 'The Introduction of Intoxicating Liquors amongst the Indians of
  the Northwest Coast.' In J. Friesen and H.K. Ralston, eds., *Historical Essays
  on British Columbia*, 44–56. Toronto: McClelland and Stewart, 1976.

Iacovetta, Franca, and Mariana Valverde, eds. *Gender Conflicts: New Essays in
  Women's History*. Toronto: University of Toronto Press, 1992.

Jones, Gareth Stedman. 'Class Expression versus Social Control?: A Critique of
  Recent Trends in the History of "Leisure".' *History Workshop Journal* 4
  (autumn 1977): 162–70.

Keller, Betty. *On the Shady Side: Vancouver 1886–1914*. Ganges, BC: Horsdal
  and Schubart, 1986.

Kennedy, Elizabeth Lapovksy, and Madeline D. Davis. *Boots of Leather, Slippers
  of Gold: The History of a Lesbian Community*. New York: Routledge, 1993.

Kent, Christopher 'Presence and Absence: History, Theory and the Working
  Class.' *Victorian Studies* 30 (spring 1986): 437–62.

– 'Victorian Social History: Post-Thompson, Post-Foucault, Postmodern.'
  Victorian Studies 40 (autumn 1996): 97–133.

Kimmel, Michael. *Manhood in America: A Cultural History*. New York: Free
  Press, 1996.

Kingsdale, Jon 'The "Poor Man's Club": Social Functions of the Urban
  Working-Class Saloon.' *American Quarterly* 25 (Oct. 1973): 472–89.

Kirkby, Diane. *Barmaids: A History of Women's Work in Pubs*. Melbourne:
  Cambridge University Press, 1997.

Lai, David Chuenyan. *Chinatowns: Towns within Cities in Canada*.Vancouver:
  UBC Press, 1988.

Lanza, Joseph. *The Cocktail: The Influence of Spirits on the American Psyche*. New York: St Martin's Press, 1995.

Lears, T.J. Jackson. 'The Concept of Cultural Hegemony: Problems and Possibilities.' *American Historical Review* 90 (1985): 567–93.

Leier, Mark. *Red Flags & Red Tape: The Making of a Labour Bureaucracy*. Toronto: University of Toronto Press, 1995.

– 'W[h]ither Labour History: Regionalism, Class, and the Writing of BC History.' *BC Studies* 111 (autumn 1996): 61–75.

Leigh, Barbara C. '"A thing so fallen, and so vile": Images of Drinking and Sexuality in Women.' *Contemporary Drug Problems* 22 (fall 1995): 415–34.

Leland, Joy. *Firewater Myths: North American Indian Drinking and Alcohol Addiction*. New Brunswick, NJ: Rutgers Center of Alcohol Studies, 1976.

Lemert, Edwin M. *Alcohol and the Northwest Coast Indians*. Berkeley: University of California Press, 1954. (University of California Publications in Culture and Society, ed. R. Centers et. al., Vol. 2, No. 6, 303–406).

Loo, Tina. 'Dan Cranmer's Potlatch: Law as Coercion, Symbol, and Rhetoric in British Columbia, 1884–1951.' *Canadian Historical Review* 73 (1992): 125–65.

– *Making Law, Order, and Authority in British Columbia, 1821–1871*. Toronto: University of Toronto Press, 1994.

Loo, Tina, and Carolyn Strange. 'The Traveling Show Menace: Contested Regulation in Turn-of-Century Ontario.' *Law and Society Review* 29 (1995): 639–67.

Macdonald, Ian, and Betty O'Keefe. *The Mulligan Affair: Top Cop on the Take*. Surrey, BC: Heritage House, 1997.

Mancall, Peter C. *Deadly Medicine: Indians and Alcohol in Early America*. Ithaca, NY: Cornell University Press, 1995.

Maracle, Brian. *Crazywater: Native Voices on Addiction and Recovery*. Toronto: Viking, 1993.

Marks, Lynne. *Revivals and Roller Rinks: Religion, Leisure, and Identity in Late-Nineteenth-Century Small-Town Ontario*. Toronto: University of Toronto Press, 1996.

Marquis, Greg. 'Vancouver Vice: The Police and the Negotiation of Morality, 1904–1935.' In *Essays in the History of Canadian Law*, Vol. 6: John McLaren and Hamar Foster, eds., *The Legal History of British Columbia and the Yukon*, 242–73. Toronto: University of Toronto Press, 1995.

May, Elaine Tyler. *Homeward Bound: American Families in the Cold War Era*. New York: Basic Books, 1988.

Maynard, Steven. 'Through a Hole in the Lavatory Wall: Homosexual Subcultures, Police Surveillance, and the Dialectics of Discovery, Toronto, 1890–1930.' *Journal of the History of Sexuality* 5 (1994): 207–42.

McBurney, Margaret, and Mary Byers. *Tavern in the Town: Early Inns and Taverns of Ontario*. Toronto: University of Toronto Press, 1987.

McDonald, Robert A.J. 'Working.' In Working Lives Collective, ed., *Working Lives: Vancouver 1886–1986*, 25–33. Vancouver: New Star Books, 1985.

– *Making Vancouver: Class, Status, and Social Boundaries, 1863–1913*. Vancouver: UBC Press, 1996.

McLaren, Angus. *The Trials of Masculinity: Policing Sexual Boundaries, 1870–1930*. Chicago: University of Chicago Press, 1997.

Miller, J.R. *Skyscrapers Hide the Heavens: A History of Indian–White Relations in Canada*. Rev. ed. Toronto: University of Toronto Press, 1991.

Moran, Bridget. *Stoney Creek Woman: The Story of Mary John*. Vancouver: Tillacum Library, 1988.

Morrison, James H., and James Moreira, eds. *Tempered by Rum: Rum in the History of the Maritime Provinces*. Porters Lake, NS: Pottersfield Press, 1988.

Murdock, Catherine Gilbert. *Domesticating Drink: Women, Men, and Alcohol in America, 1870–1940*. Baltimore, Md.: Johns Hopkins University Press, 1998.

Murphy, Mary. *Mining Cultures: Men, Women and Leisure in Butte, 1914–41*. Urbana: University of Illinois Press, 1997.

Noel, Jan. *Canada Dry: Temperance Crusades before Confederation*. Toronto: University of Toronto Press, 1995.

Owram, Doug. *Born at the Right Time: A History of the Baby-Boom Generation*. Toronto: University of Toronto Press, 1996.

Palmer, Bryan D. *Descent into Discourse: The Reification of Language and the Writing of Social History*. Philadelphia: Temple University Press, 1990.

– 'Critical Theory, Historical Materialism, and the Ostensible End of Marxism: The Poverty of Theory Revisited.' *International Review of Social History* 38 (1993): 133–62.

Panitch, Leo, ed. *The Canadian State: Political Economy and Political Power*. Toronto: University of Toronto Press, 1977.

Park, J. 'Only "Those Women": Women and the Control of Alcohol in New Zealand.' *Contemporary Drug Problems* 17 (1990): 221–50.

Parr, Joy. 'Gender History and Historical Practice.' *Canadian Historical Review* 76 (Sept. 1995): 354–76.

– 'Shopping for a Good Stove: A Parable about Gender, Design, and the Market.' In Joy Parr, ed., *A Diversity of Women in Ontario, 1945–1980*, 75–97. Toronto: University of Toronto Press, 1995.

Paulson, Don, with Roger Simpson. *An Evening in the Garden of Allah: A Gay Cabaret in Seattle*. New York: Columbia University Press, 1996.

Peiss, Kathy L. *Cheap Amusements: Working Women and Leisure in Turn-of-the-Century New York*. Philadelphia: Temple University Press, 1986.

Penn, Donna. 'The Sexualized Woman: The Lesbian, the Prostitute, and the

Containment of Female Sexuality in Postwar America.' In Joanne Meyer-
    witz, ed., *Not June Cleaver: Women and Gender in Postwar America, 1945–1960*,
    358–81. Philadelphia: Temple University Press, 1994.
Pettigrew, Margaret, and Ginny Sikeman, prods. Videocassette. *Forbidden Love:
    The Unabashed Stories of Lesbian Lives*. Directed by Aerlyn Weissman and
    Lynne Fernie. 85 minutes. National Film Board of Canada, 1992.
Phillips, Walter. '"Six O'clock Swill": The Introduction of Early Closing of
    Hotel Bars in Australia.' *Historical Studies* 19 (1980): 250–66.
Pope, Peter. 'Fish into Wine: The Historical Anthropology of Demand for
    Alcohol in Seventeenth-Century Newfoundland.' *Histoire sociale/Social
    History* 27 (Nov. 1994): 261–78. Reprinted in Blocker and Warsh, eds., *The
    Changing Face of Drink*, 43–64.
Powers, Madelon. *Faces along the Bar: Lore and Order in the Workingman's
    Saloon, 1870–1920*. Chicago: University of Chicago Press, 1998.
Prestwich, Patricia E. 'The Regulation of Drinking: New Work in the Social
    History of Alcohol.' *Contemporary Drug Problems* 21 (fall 1994): 365–72.
Prothero, Iorwerth. *Radical Artisans in England and France, 1830–1870*. Cam-
    bridge: Cambridge University Press, 1997.
Quetel, Claude. *History of Syphilis*. Baltimore, Md.: Johns Hopkins University
    Press, 1992. (Originally published as *Le Mal de Naples: histoire de la syphilis*,
    Paris: Seghers, 1986.)
Regehr, Ernie. *Perceptions of Apartheid: The Churches and Political Change in
    South Africa*. Kitchener, Ont.: Between the Lines, 1979.
Robinson, Daniel J. and David Kimmel. 'The Queer Career of Homosexual
    Security Vetting in Cold War Canada.' *Canadian Historical Review* 75 (Sept.
    1994): 319–45.
Rosenzweig, Roy. *Eight Hours for What We Will: Workers and Leisure in an
    Industrial City, 1870–1920*. New York: Cambridge University Press,
    1983.
Roy, Patricia E. *A White Man's Province: British Columbia Politicians and Chinese
    and Japanese Immigrants, 1858–1914*. Vancouver: UBC Press, 1989.
Rutherford, Paul. *A Victorian Authority: The Daily Press in Nineteenth-Century
    Canada*. Toronto: University of Toronto Press, 1982.
Said, Edward W. *Orientalism*. New York: Random House, 1978.
Sangster, Joan. 'Incarcerating "Bad Girls": The Regulation of Sexuality
    through the Female Refuges Act in Ontario, 1920–1945.' *Journal of the
    History of Sexuality* 7 (1996): 239–75.
Schlase, Megan. 'Liquor and the Indian Post WWII.' *B.C. Historical News* 29
    (spring 1996): 26–9.
Scott, Joan W. *Gender and the Politics of History*. New York: Columbia Univer-
    sity Press, 1988.

Sheriff, Peta E. 'State Theory, Social Science, and Governmental Commissions.' *American Behavioral Scientist* 26 (1983): 669–80.

Single, Eric, and Thomas Storm, eds. *Public Drinking and Public Policy*. (Proceedings of a Symposium on Observational Studies held at Banff, Alberta, 26–28 April 1984). Toronto: Alcoholism and Drug Addiction Research Foundation, 1985.

Smart, Reginald G., and Alan C. Ogborne. *Northern Spirits: A Social History of Alcohol in Canada*. 2nd ed. Toronto: Addiction Research Foundation, 1996.

Sommer, R. 'The Isolated Drinker in the Edmonton Beer Parlor.' *Quarterly Journal on the Studies of Alcohol* 26 (1965): 95–110.

Spain, Daphne. *Gendered Spaces*. Chapel Hill: University of North Carolina Press, 1992.

Spence, Ruth. *Prohibition in Canada*. Toronto: Dominion Alliance, 1919.

Storm, Thomas, and R.E. Cutler. 'Observations of Drinking in Natural Settings: Vancouver Beer Parlors and Cocktail Lounges.' *Journal of Studies on Alcohol* 42 (1981): 972–97.

Strange, Carolyn. *Toronto's Girl Problem: The Perils and Pleasures of the City, 1880–1930*. Toronto: University of Toronto Press, 1995.

Strange, Carolyn, and Tina Loo. 'Spectacular Justice: The Circus on Trial, and the Trial as Circus, Picton, 1903.' *Canadian Historical Review* 77 (June 1996): 159–84.

– *Making Good: Law and Moral Regulation in Canada, 1867–1939*. Toronto: University of Toronto Press, 1997.

Strong-Boag, Veronica. *The Parliament of Women: The National Council of Women of Canada, 1893–1929*. Ottawa: National Museum of Man, 1976.

– *The New Day Recalled: Lives of Girls and Women in English Canada, 1919–1939*. Markham, Ont.: Penguin, 1988.

– 'Home Dreams: Women and the Suburban Experiment in Canada, 1945–1960.' *Canadian Historical Review* 72 (Dec. 1991): 471–504.

Thompson, E.P. *The Making of the English Working Class*. Rev. ed. London: Penguin, 1980.

Thompson, Peter. *Rum Punch and Revolution: Taverngoing and Public Life in Eighteenth-Century Philadelphia*. Philadelphia: University of Pennsylvania Press, 1999.

Tlusty, Beverly Ann. 'Gender and Alcohol Use in Early Modern Augsburg.' *Histoire sociale/Social History* 27 (Nov. 1994): 241–60.

Tobias, John L. 'Protection, Civilization, Assimilation: An Outline History of Canada's Indian Policy.' In Ian A.L. Getty and Antoine S. Lussier, eds., *As Long as the Sun Shines and Water Flows: A Reader in Canadian Native Studies*, 39–55. Vancouver: University of British Columbia Press, 1983.

Trower, Peter. *Deadman's Ticket: A Novel of the Streets and the Woods*. Madeira Park, BC: Harbour Publishing, 1996.

Valverde, Mariana. *The Age of Light, Soap, and Water: Moral Reform in English Canada, 1885–1925*. Toronto: McClelland and Stewart, 1991.

– '"When the Mother of the Race is Free": Race, Reproduction, and Sexuality in First-Wave Feminism.' In Iacovetta and Valverde, eds., *Gender Conflicts*, 3–26.

– 'Editor's Introduction.' *Canadian Journal of Sociology* 19 no. 2 (1994): vii–xii.

– 'Moral Capital.' *Canadian Journal of Law and Society* 9 (1994): 213–32.

– comp. *Radically Rethinking Regulation: Workshop Report*. Toronto: Centre of Criminology, University of Toronto, 1994.

– *Diseases of the Will: Alcohol and the Dilemmas of Freedom*. Cambridge: Cambridge University Press, 1998.

Ward, W. Peter. *White Canada Forever: Popular Attitudes and Public Policy toward Orientals in British Columbia*. Montreal: McGill-Queen's University, 1978.

Warsh, Cheryl Krasnick, ed. *Drink in Canada: Historical Essays*. Montreal: McGill-Queen's University Press, 1993.

Weiss, Gillian 'The Brightest Women of Our Land: Vancouver Clubwomen 1919–1928.' In Barbara K. Latham and Roberta J. Pazdro, eds., *Not Just Pin Money: Selected Essays on the History of Women's Work in British Columbia*, 199–207. Victoria: Camosun College, 1984.

Williams, Donald H. 'Commercialized Prostitution and Venereal-Disease Control.' *Canadian Public Health Journal* 31 (1940): 461–72.

– 'Canada's National Health and Venereal Disease Control.' *Canadian Journal of Public Health* 3 (1943): 261–6.

– 'The Facilitation Process and Venereal Disease Control: A Study of Source Finding and Suppression of Facilitation in the Greater Vancouver Area.' Canadian *Journal of Public Health* 34 (1943): 393–405.

Illustration Credits

Index

Abbotsford Hotel, 41
Aberdeen, Lord and Lady, 16
Aboriginal people: and alcohol, permitted access to, 104; –, prohibition of access to, 12, 94, 95, 99; attempted assimilation of, 94; and beer parlours, admission to, 99–100; –, intoxication incidents in, 102, 103; –, objection to, by white patrons, 100–1, 102; –, refusal of service to, 12, 79, 81, 130; campaign for equal drinking rights, 97–104; and definition of Indian, 95–6; drinking, attitudes towards, 104; enfranchisement, by giving up Indian status, 94; 'firewater myth,' 93–4, 95; as flexible category, 104, 130; liquor permits, denial of, 94, 95; as minors in law, 94; 'passing' as white in beer parlours, 12, 80, 96; as servicemen in foreign canteens, 98–9; women, in beer parlours, 85, 96–7, 100; –, in company of white men, 85. *See also* Indian Act
Adams, Mary Louise, 9, 23
African Canadians. *See* blacks

alcohol: consumption increase, after 1945, 110; sold as medicine during prohibition, 18. *See also* beer; liquor
Alcohol Research Council, 113
American Hotel, 84
Anchor Hotel, 32, 38
Anderlini, I., 33
Anderson, Kay, 134
Angelus Hotel, 65
Anti-Beer League, 54
Ashforth, Adam, 134
Asian people: exclusion, from Canadian citizenship, 12, 79, 81, 105; –, from holding beer parlour licences, 12–13, 86, 105, –, from ownership of beer parlours, 79, 81, 86, 130, –, from working in beer parlours, 79, 86, 130; hotel ownership by, 87; as infrequent patrons of beer parlours, 88; voting rights, 86. *See also* Chinese people; Japanese people

bar. *See* stand-up bar
bartenders. *See* tapmen
Bartenders Blitz charity event, 115

serving, 120; creation of, 30; as defender of beer parlours, before Liquor Inquiry Commission, 114–15. *See also* Local 676; tapmen; waiters, in beer parlours

blacks: as beer parlour patrons, 13, 105; as railway employees, 82, 83; refusal of service to, in beer parlours, 79, 82–4; as residents of Hogan's Alley, 83

Blocker, Jack, 3–4, 7

Bonner, Robert, 33

bookmaking. *See* gambling, in beer parlours

bootlegging, during prohibition, 18, 87

Boston saloons, and gender segregation, 6

Brennan, Thomas, 4

brewers: and Liquor Inquiry Commission, 116–17; loan guarantees for beer parlours, 116–17; and 'tied houses,' 117

British Columbia, government of. *See* Government Liquor Act; Liquor Control Board (LCB); Liquor Inquiry Commission (1952); plebiscites, on liquor policy

British Columbia Hotels Association (BCHA): banning of women from beer parlours, 53–4, 95; class issue in beer parlours, 46–7; defence of beer parlours during Second World War, 42; and gambling in beer parlours, 39–41; and Liquor Inquiry Commission (1952), 115–16; lobby for licensed premises, 21; and short service of beer, 44, 45, 46, 49; support for end to prohibition, 20

British Columbia Prohibition Act, 18

British Columbia Prohibition Association (BCPA): and 1924 plebiscite on public drinking, 20; on banning of women from beer parlours, 54, 95

British Columbia Temperance League (BCTL): objection to plebiscite on public drinking, 113; rating of Vancouver beer parlours, 66; request for closure of beer parlours during Second World War, 42

Broadway Hotel, 22

Burde, R.J. (Major), 89, 91

Burrard Hotel, 92

cabarets: as 'bottle clubs,' 111–12; licensing of, 112, 119; promotion of cocktails, 111

Canadian Brotherhood of Railway Employees, and Liquor Inquiry Commission (1952), 115

Canadian Congress of Labour (CCL), objection to wartime beer restrictions, 43–4

Canadian National Railways (CNR), 83

Canadian Pacific Railway (CPR), 83

Canadian Temperance Federation: on 1952 plebiscite on public drinking, 114; request to stop sale of liquor during Second World War, 42

Canning, Kathleen, 8

capital, and state interests, 132

Castle Hotel, 19, 69

Cave (cabaret), 112

Cecil Hotel, 91

Chamberland, Line, 71, 72

Chauncey, George, 27, 70

prohibition, 18, 87; business licences for, 19; legislation regulating, 17–19. *See also* Liquor Control
Board (LCB)
Liquor Control Board (LCB): on beer
parlours as source of venereal
disease, 61–2; corruption, accusations of, 25, 26, 117–19; discrimination against mixed-race couples, 13, 84–5; family allowance
cheques, prohibition of cashing
in liquor stores, 67–8; fines for
serving minors in beer parlours,
89–90, 92–3; gambling in beer
parlours, prohibition of, 39–41;
government liquor stores, 19;
liquor inspectors, 35–6; and
political patronage, 117–19;
regulation enforcement, 25, 26;
segregation of women in beer
parlours, 25, 55, 57; toleration of
gay men and lesbians in beer
parlours, 12, 70, 75–6, 129; on
undesirability of women in beer
parlours, 51
Liquor Inquiry Commission (1952),
114–19, 134
liquor permits, and purchasing
rights in government store, 94, 95
Local 676: argument for two-glass
limit per serving, 120; as defender
of beer parlours, before Liquor
Inquiry Commission, 114–15;
defender of hotel monopoly on
sale of beer, 30; disciplinary action
for drinking on the job, 32–3, 48;
history, 30; on members' regulating beer parlour violence, 39;
objection to women servers in beer
parlours, 120; *Official Handbook,*

29; participation in March of
Dimes charity, 115
Loo, Tina, 8, 131
Lotus Hotel, 38, 40, 87
Low, Rose (Mrs), 33, 82

McClung, Nellie, 19
McGugan, Donald (Col.), 26
McIntyre, R.J. (Rev.), 54, 87, 95
Mackintosh, Carol Ritchie, 72
Main Hotel, 67, 69, 83, 87, 92
Mancall, Peter, 93–4
Manitoba Liquor Inquiry Commis-
sion, 121
Manson, Alex M., 20, 53
Marquis, Greg, 22–3
Marr Hotel, 97
Martin Hotel, 79, 80, 82, 84
Martinique Hotel, 33, 66
Massachusetts saloons, 5
Melbourne Hotel, 35, 97, 99
minors: fines for drinking in beer
parlours, 92; as flexible category,
104, 130; girls, in beer parlours,
90–1, 92; identification, presenta-
tion of, 92; prohibited in beer
parlours, 12, 79, 81, 88–93, 130
mixed-race couples: definition, 13,
80, 85, 105, 130; unwanted in beer
parlours, 12–13, 79, 80, 84–5, 105,
130
Moderation League: advocacy
of government sale of liquor,
18; support for end to prohibition,
20
Moffat, John, 40
Monks, Noel, 107, 124–5
Montana, drinking policies, 7
moral regulation: of beer parlours, 3,
10, 11, 128; and cleanliness, 73–4;

Stratford Hotel, 83, 86
Swanson, Cecil (Rev.), 114
Sylvia Hotel, 123

tapmen: as beer parlour managers,
34; duties, 31; treating of, 5
Tattersall, T.D. (Mrs), 56
taverns, Parisian, 4–5
temperance movement: and 'firewater myth' of Aboriginal lack of
alcohol tolerance, 95; government
lobbying during Second World
War, 42; objection to public drinking, 76; objection to saloons, 127;
rejection of plebiscite on public
drinking, 113; use of scientific
discourse, 126. *See also* prohibitionists
Thorne, Chuck, 99
tied houses, 117
Tobias, John, 94
transgendered people, in beer parlours, 12, 72, 75–6, 129
treating: by beer parlour licensees,
prohibition of, 120; and male
culture, 5; seen as promoting
excessive consumption, 68; of
tapmen, 5
Tremont House, 17
Trower, Peter, 22, 69
Tweedsmuir Hotel (Burns Lake, BC),
100, 102

unions. *See* Beverage Dispensers
Union (BDU); Local 676
United Church of Canada,
Vancouver East Presbytery, 53
Uphill, Tom, 20, 123

Valverde, Mariana: on beer parlour

prohibitions, 88; on lack of definition of problem with saloon bars,
122; on licence holder as object of
regulation, 27; on liquor restrictions and definition of Indian, 94;
on regulation of drinking environment, 23; on shift in drinking
ethics after 1945, 110
Vancouver, BC: downtown, as
disreputable area, 22–3; vote for
sale of beer, 20–1
Vancouver and District Labour
Council (V&DLC): complaint
about short service of beer, 44;
and Liquor Inquiry Commission
(1952), 115; objection to wartime
beer restrictions, 43
Vancouver Breweries, 116
Vancouver Council of Churches, 113
Vancouver Council of Women
(VCW): objection to beer parlours,
55–6; as silent on women in beer
parlours, 55
Vancouver Trades and Labour
Council (VLTC), 30
Vanport Hotel, 69–70
venereal disease: and beer parlour
segregation of unattached men
and women, 57, 60; condoms,
illegal under Criminal Code, 58;
infection rates of armed forces
(First World War), 58; legislation
and regulation, 58–9, 62, 132;
prostitutes as alleged source of,
57–62, 76–7; seen as sabotaging
war effort, 58, 61
Venereal Diseases Suppression Act
(1919), 58–9, 62
veterans' clubs, consumption of
liquor in, 19–20

STUDIES IN GENDER AND HISTORY

General editors: Franca Iacovetta and Karen Dubinsky